# The Computer Animation Dictionary

Robi Roncarelli

# The Computer Animation Dictionary

Including Related Terms Used in Computer
Graphics, Film and Video, Production, and
Desktop Publishing

Springer-Verlag
New York Berlin Heidelberg
London Paris Tokyo Hong Kong

Robi Roncarelli
217 George Street
Toronto, Ontario
Canada M5A 2M9

On the front cover: Tinny, the wind-up star of Pixar's 1988 Oscar-winning short film *Tin Toy*. © 1988 Pixar. The film is the first work of computer animation ever to receive an Academy Award.

Library of Congress Cataloging-in-Publication Data
Roncarelli, Robi.
    The computer animation dictionary : including related terms used
in computer graphics, film and video, production, and desktop
publishing / Robi Roncarelli.
        p.    cm.
    ISBN 0-387-97022-3 (alk. paper)
    1. Computer animation—Dictionaries.   I. Title.
    TR897.5.R66   1989
700—dc20                                                    89-11300

Printed on acid-free paper.

Camera-ready copy supplied by author.
Printed and bound by R.R. Donnelley & Sons, Harrisonburg, VA.
Printed in the United States of America.

9 8 7 6 5 4 3 2 1

ISBN 0-387-97022-3 Springer-Verlag New York Berlin Heidelberg
ISBN 3-540-97022-3 Springer-Verlag Berlin Heidelberg New York

# Preface

*Dr Alvy Ray Smith*
*Executive Vice President, Pixar*

The polyglot language of computer animation has arisen piecemeal as a collection of terms borrowed from geometry, film, video, painting, conventional animation, computer graphics, computer science, and publishing - in fact, from every older art or science which has anything to do with pictures and picture making. Robi Roncarelli, who has already demonstrated his foresight by formally identifying a nascent industry and addressing his Computer Animation Newsletter to it, here again makes a useful contribution to it by codifying its jargon. My pleasure in reading his dictionary comes additionally from the many historical notes sprinkled throughout and from surprise entries such as the one referring to Zimbabwe.

Just as Samuel Johnson's dictionary of the English language was a major force in stabilizing the spelling of English, perhaps this one will serve a similar purpose for computer animation. Two of my pets are "color" for "colour" and "modeling" "modelling", under the rule that the shorter accepted spelling is always preferable. [Robi, are you reading this?] [Yes, Alvy!] Now I commend this book to you, whether you be a newcomer or an oldtimer. Just to get started, do you know the difference between "pixellization" and "pixilation"?

Alvy Ray Smith
Pixar
San Rafael, California
February 28, 1989

# Preface

*Paul Brown*
*Director, Computer Image Program*
*Swinburne Institute of Technology*

As the co-founder of Digital Pictures, one of England's leading computer animation studios, and now as an educator trying to introduce computer graphics and animation to a wide variety of arts and science students, I'm constantly reminded that a major problem is jargon! Jargon is useful - it allows those of us on the inside to communicate often complex concepts and methods briefly and efficiently. But to those on the outside jargon is a stumbling block to understanding that has, in my experience, ruined several commercial computer animation sequences and helped others go over-budget and over-time.

So this new book by Robi Roncarelli is particularly welcome. Robi, for the past five years, has been providing an essential service to both industry and academia by publishing Pixel - The Computer Animation Newsletter and, more recently The Roncarelli Report - the annual market review and forecast.

In the Computer Animation Dictionary he shares his knowledge of the jargon of this new and exciting business. So now we have no excuses and anyone who wants to know what a Perturbed Normal or a WIMP is, or what a Phong Shader does, need look no further. In addition to Computer Animation there are terms from publishing, film and video special effects, telecommunications, general computing and other affiliated areas which emphasise the continuing integration of disciplines that the computer revolution has enabled.

Paul Brown
Swinburne Institute
Melbourne, Australia
March 5, 1989

# Introduction

**The Computer Animation Dictionary** is a direct response to the many requests I have received over the past five years for a reference source of this type.

While there have been descriptions, or lexicons, of words used in this industry published from time-to-time in various magazines and publications, and also by various equipment and software systems suppliers and manufacturers, there has never been one concise, standard source for these descriptions and explanations. And the problem is escalating as our industry changes and grows, and the user-base rapidly expands.

It isn't a new need. One of the features in the early issues of *PIXEL - THE COMPUTER ANIMATION NEWSLETTER,* when I started publishing it over five years ago, was an on-going *"lexicon"* of computer animation industry terms in use at that time. Many of these terms have since changed, many are still with us. And we have an increasing number of new terms and words to keep up-to-date with as the use of the technology expands into new areas.

In compiling this **Dictionary,** I have used as reference information, descriptions and explanations from a great many sources within the general computer, computer graphics and animation, and electronic publishing industries, and my own "dictionary database" which I have been building over the past several years. It started out as a "lexicon of computer animation industry terms" which we were going to publish as an adjunct to our **Newsletter.** But then, as the industry exploded, it became too big.

In addition to computer animation and computer graphics terms, there also were questions about computer terms in general, as computers and their operations were basic to all our graphics usages. Then, there was the question of film and video production terms that were being encountered by people involved in computer animation production. The rapidly expanding use of *desktop publishing* created another user group involved with much the same equipment, similar software, and problems. And so, as the **Dictionary** grew too big for our own publishing resources, so too did our potential user market and its demand for this information. Enter Springer-Verlag, a company well versed in responding to the publishing needs of the computer graphics industry, and this little book is the result. We hope it is a handy reference tool for you.

In compiling all the terms included between these covers, we had to determine how far we would go in those areas beyond direct computer graphics and animation use. The film industry has a language all its own, as do the graphics printing and typesetting industries, but many of their terms are not directly applicable to our needs. We have accordingly only included the terms used in those areas which we have encountered as commonly used in computer graphics, animation and desktop publishing.

Where a word, or words, appear in *italics*, it indicates that they are covered, or cross-referenced, under their own individual headings elsewhere in the **Dictionary**. We have tried to judiciously include some terms and references which may now be considered as becoming outdated, but which a user could well come across in their reading or daily work. We have also included various historical and general interest information because we believe that having a feeling for the history of our industry, and the people involved, will give readers a better understanding and appreciation of its youthful vitality.

But we have <u>not</u> tried to be <u>exhaustive.</u> This book is **NOT** an encyclopedia. Rather, we have designed this book to fill the growing global need for a quick, handy and concise <u>reference dictionary,</u> with added explanations beyond simple descriptions when they seemed warranted. Whenever we encountered different spellings for a word, we always opted for the shorter, usually American, form, because that is the general global language of computers. However, there are regional, or national, usages or spellings for some words and terms which we have indicated.

One of the problems in getting this book to press is the very vitality of our industry. New terms and usages keep coming up. Even as my data file keeps growing, we had to draw the line in the early part of 1989 in order to make our targeted introduction date. So we'll try to keep it updated for you from time to time.

This is probably the only book you will ever see on the subject of computer graphics and animation, that is devoid of pictures and diagrams. This was a considered decision, resulting from our desire to keep the **Dictionary** small enough for use as a handy, portable, reference book.

However, an illustrated edition is being contemplated.

Many people helped, directly and indirectly, with the preparation of this material. Besides the constant support and assistance of the people in my own office, led by my wife and co-worker Denise Desrosiers, I would like to particularly thank Paul Brown and Alvy Ray Smith, whose friendship I hope I haven't strained too much by giving them the task of checking the manuscript from both an academic and industry technical correctness standpoint. Their much appreciated added input, comments and suggestions have contributed greatly to this work. I would also like to thank my friend and associate Dan Jex, whose council on this book's growth and preparation was always helpful, and Paul Brown's partner and research assistant, Judith Crow, who was an invaluable help to him in correcting and notating the manuscript.

And finally, I dedicate this book to Daniella and Martina, may they never stop asking "why?"

Robi Roncarelli
Toronto, Canada
March 10, 1989

**AA** - *Author's alterations.*

**A&B rolls** - Two rolls of film (or videotape) which have individual shots, or sequences, placed alternately, first on the A Roll, then on the B Roll. When printed, the A&B rolls are coordinated to produce a single roll of film. The use of A&B rolls enables filmed scenes to overlap from one scene to the next with dissolves, fades and other effects.

**Abekas** - Digital disc recorder in various models that can store many seconds of animation frames or single video images so they can be played back in *real time*. Manufactured by Abekas Video Corporation.

**absolute point** - An individually addressable point at a specific position on the display screen.

**absolute vector** - A line segment drawn from the current position to an absolute point.

**academy aperture** - Defines the size of the film frame aperture gate on standard (not wide screen) 35mm film. 21.95mm wide by 16.0mm high.

**access time** - The time interval between the moment when *data* is called for from a *computer's memory* or storage *device*, and its delivery to the *processor (CPU)*, screen etc.

**access** - To locate and have entry to an area of main or auxiliary *computer memory* for the purpose of storing *data* and/or retrieving it from that point.

**achromatic color** - A color that is found along the grey scale from black to white.

**AC** - *Author's alterations* or corrections.

**ACM** - Association for Computing Machinery.

**ACS** - Australian Computer Society.

**Ada** - A USA Department of Defense procedural *programming language*, which has also been adopted by the *American National Standards Institute (ANSI)*, designed for use in certain military *computer* systems. It is oriented toward batch and time-sharing systems, and is now also beginning to be used for general computing applications. Named for British mathematician Lady Ada Lovelace.

**ADC** - *Analog to digital conversion.*

**address** - The location, or index, of a *word* of *data* in *memory* storage, where it can be found if one wants to retrieve that specific bit of data for any reason.

**addressability** - The smallest discrete unit by which a *display* element can be defined, and to which the *hardware* responds.

**addressable point** - A position on the viewing area of a *CRT screen* to which the CRT's beam may be directed, as specified by its coordinates.

**ADO** - Ampex Digital Optics. A *digital effects* device that has built-in programs to manipulate pre-recorded or camera-grabbed images in three-dimensional (3-D) space via flips, tumbles, compression, expansion, at varying degrees or rates. The term "ADO" has become a generic reference to all *devices* that can perform these tasks.

**aerial image** - A method of projecting an image for reproduction in which the image is focused through a set of condenser lenses directly onto the photographing camera.

**AFCET** - Association Francaise pour la Cybernetique Economique et Technique.

**AFIPS** - American Federation of Information Processing Societies.

**agate line** - A unit of measurement for specifying newspaper advertising space, which is defined as 1/4 of a column inch.

**AICA** - Associazione Italiana Per Il Calcolo Automatico.

**AIEE** - American Institute of Electrical Engineers.

**airbrush** - An extremely fine paint spray-gun. In graphics, a term denoting a soft, diffused treatment of an image. Computer *paint* systems have various "brush styles" that can pick-up color from a *palette*, or from portions of the image, to apply to the image.

**AIX** - *IBM's* version of the *Unix* operating system.

**ALGOL** - Algorithmic Language. A high-level *computer programming language* developed by American and European scientists.

**algorithm** - a "recipe" or set of instructions for solving a *computer* problem via a series of step-by-step computer programming commands, independent of any specific computer *language* or computer *system*.

**Alias/1** - A high-level, three-dimensional, *workstation* based *computer animation* production, design and rendering system with sophisticated capabilities, manufactured by Alias Research Inc. Now also available as an upgraded Alias/2 system.

**aliasing** - The generally unwanted visual effect in *computer* generated images caused by insufficient sampling *resolution* or inadequate *filtering* to completely define the object, most commonly seen as a jagged or "stepped" edge along the object's boundary, or along a line. Temporal aliasing can impart a juddering movement to an object. See *anti-aliasing* and *motion blur*.

**Alias Research** - Manufacturer of the *Alias/1* and Alias/2 computer animation systems.

**alpha channel** - One of four channels of information associated with each *pixel* of an image (the other three are Red, Green and Blue - *RGB*). The *alpha channel* carries additional information for compositing the pixel's RGB elements, such as degree of transparency. *Alpha* represents area coverage of the pixel.

**alphanumeric** - *Data* that consists of letters and numbers.

**ALU** - *Arithmetic and Logic Unit.*

**AmigaDOS** - The operating system for the Commodore Amiga line of *personal computers*.

**AM/FM** - Automated Mapping/Facilities Management. A type of system used for map production.

**analog** - The characteristic of varying continuously along a scale, as opposed to increasing or decreasing in fixed increments (as in *digital*). A continuous, rather than discrete, means of analyzing a signal or processing information. An *analog computer* or electronic system is based on relating degrees of information. *Analog* graphic/video systems vary in quality according to the number of *scanlines* per inch.

**analog animation** - *Computer animation* by *raster* manipulation, usually done with *Scanimate* computers. One of the first commercially viable forms of two-dimensional computer animation, now replaced by *digital* animation techniques.

**analog to digital conversion (ADC)** - The process of converting *analog* signals to *digital* signals.

**analog-stroke** - An *analog* technique for moving a *CRT beam* across the face of a *display screen*. Commonly used in high-performance character and vector generators, the *analog-stroke* method is an order of magnitude faster than comparable *digital* techniques.

**ANIMA** - A three-dimensional, real time, *computer animation* system developed by Charles Csuri in 1975, at Ohio State University.

**ANIMA II** - A three-dimensional, color, *computer animation* system developed by R Hackathorn in 1977, at Ohio State University.

**animatic** - A rough, usually incomplete, sequence of images photographed or recorded to give a sense of action, timing and/or composition of a proposed animation. Usually produced for testing prior to the final version.

**animation** - Producing the illusion of movement in a film/video by photographing, or otherwise recording, a series of single frames, each showing incremental changes in the position of the subject images, which when shown in sequence, at high speed, give the illusion of movement. The individual frames can be produced by a variety of techniques from *computer* generated images, to hand-drawn *cels*.

**animation cycle** - A series of *animation* frames that form a completed movement sequence, which can then be repeated (re-cycled) a number of times to extend a movement without having to re-draw the frames, ie: a *"walk cycle"*.

**animation rostrum** - See *animation stand*.

**animation stand** - A device for recording flat animation drawings, cels, etc onto film or video, one frame at a time. The cels are positioned via a series of registration pins on a flat table which can be moved horizontally in relation to the camera. The camera is suspended on a vertical post above the table and can be moved up and down in relation to the table. The movement of the artwork and the camera, and their relationship, are now generally controlled by a *computer*. The British call this device an *animation rostrum*.

**animator** - An artist who uses the techniques of frame-by-frame *animation* to give his artwork the illusion of movement. Also, the operator of a *computer animation* system.

**ANIMATOR** - A two-dimensional, interactive film *animation* system developed at the University of Pennsylvania in 1971.

**answer print** - The first fully completed, with synchronised sound tracks, final version film print or video recording of a production.

**ANSI** - American National Standards Institute.

**anti-aliasing** - *Software* or *programs* designed to correct the *aliasing*, or "stepped" appearance, of diagonal or curved lines and borders on a *raster* display. A variety of techniques have been developed for this, one technique involves averaging intensities between neighbouring *pixels* along edges of objects in the scene, which visually softens the jagged effect. Another technique sums area coverage within the pixel. See *alpha channel, dither*.

**Antics** - A two-dimensional, keyframe based *computer animation* software system, particularly designed to emulate traditional-style animation. It now has a three-dimensional overlay available. Developed by Alan Kitching, Grove Park Studio, in 1973.

**ANTTS** - Animated Things Through Space. A complex three-dimensional *computer animation* system developed by a group under the direction of Charles Csuri in 1979, at Ohio State University.

**API** - Associacao Portuguesa de Informatica.

**APL** - A Programming Language. A high-level *computer programming language* for mathematical and scientific computations.

**Apollo** - A range of graphic *workstations* manufactured by Apollo Computer Inc.

**AppleTalk** - Apple Computer's proprietary communications architecture for the Macintosh computer.

**application** - A task to be performed by a *computer program* or *system*, such as graphic arts, animation, design, architecture, business graphics, etc.

**application program** - A *computer program* which performs a complete, useful function in a specialized area, as opposed to a subroutine, or subroutines, that perform part of a larger job, eg: a *paint system*, or a *word processing program*.

**architecture** - The way in which *hardware* and *software* interact to provide the system requirement. The overall "structure" of the *computer system*.

**Ardent** - Ardent Computer Corporation, manufacturers of the Titan line of graphics *supercomputers*.

**area composition** - The spatial positioning of typographic or graphic elements onto film or paper, thereby eliminating cutting and pasting of the individual typeset elements.

**arithmetic and logic unit (ALU)** - That part of a *processor (CPU)* which performs calculations as instructed to by the control unit. It can be either a single *microprocessor chip*, or one or more *circuit boards*.

**arithmetic processor/co-processor** - A computer *processor chip* designed specifically to handle arithmetic functions, in conjunction with and under the instructions of, the *central processing unit (CPU)* or chip. The addition of an *arithmetic processor* will greatly speed-up a *computer's* ability to perform the many calculations required for graphics modeling and animation.

**arguments** - Variables evaluated by a *program* to determine a result.

**array** - An organized set or *data* structure. An *array* of numbers might be one-dimensional (*vector*), two-dimensional (*matrix*), or three dimensional. *Arrays* permit repetitive methods to be used in computer processes for greater speed and efficiency.

**ARTA** - An interactive, two-dimensional *computer animation* system developed by L Mezei and A Zivian in 1971, at the University of Toronto.

**artificial intelligence (AI)** - The scientific field concerned with creating *computer systems* that can achieve "human" intellectual faculties such as the abilities to perceive, reason and learn.

**Artstar** - *Computer* graphics system with three-dimensional animation capabilities manufactured by Colorgraphics Systems.

**ASA** - American Standards Association (speed). A system used for rating the "speed", or sensitivity of photographic film emulsion to light.

**ASAS** - Actor/Scriptor Animation System. A powerful *computer animation* system developed by Craig Reynolds in 1982, and used by *Triple I*.

**ascender** - The vertical portion of a lower case alphabetic character which extends above the body of lower case characters, eg: "b" and "d".

**ASCII** - American Standard Code of Information Interchange. Commonly-used code for the representation of alphanumeric and other characters and commands on *computers*. Established by the American Standards Association, the 7-bit ASCII code offers 128 characters, the 8-bit ASCII code offers 256.

**aspect ratio** - In film, the ratio of width to height of a film or video frame. In *computer graphics*, the ratio of width to height of the horizontal and vertical *pixels*.

**assembler** - A *program* that translates the alphanumeric files written in *assembly language* into *binary machine language*.

**assembly language** - An adjunct to *machine language* that makes *programming* easier by using *mnemonic* instructions that translate into *opcodes*.

**asynchronous communication** - Method of communicating between *computers* using telephone and communications lines. Because the transmitter and receiver are not synchronised, each character transmitted is preceded by a special "start" bit, and followed by one, or two, "stop" bits.

**attribute** - The property of a displayed entity, ie: its color or intensity.

**Aurora** - Two-dimensional and three-dimensional computer graphics, animation and paint systems manufactured by Aurora Systems, which is now owned by *Chyron*.

**author's alterations (AA/AC)** - An alteration, or correction, or change of original copy or instructions made by the author.

**auxiliary storage** - A peripheral device, such as a *magnetic tape*, magnetic *disc* or *optical disc* upon which computerized *data* can be stored, as opposed to a computer's internal storage capacity.

**AVA 3** - *Computer* paint and video graphics system manufactured by Ampex Corporation.

**AVIOS** - American Voice Input/Output Society.

**axis** - The *line* around which an *object rotates*. The zero reference line in a *coordinate* system.

**background** - The area behind the main actors, or subject matter, in a scene, whether filmed in live action, or produced as a *computer* frame.

**background program (or task)** - A lower priority *program* that can be executed when higher priority tasks are not being performed.

**back lit** - A technique in which the graphics and/or animation are produced on translucent materials and placed on a *light box* for filming. The colors and/or effects produced are more saturated than with standard top-lighting.

**backup copy** - A duplicate or protection copy of *data* or *software* that is made in case the original is destroyed.

**band** - A range of frequencies.

**bandwidth** - The speed of information, typically measured in millions of *bytes* per second (MB/s). A critical parameter of *computer* performance. In telecommunications, *bandwidth* is used to describe the extent of the frequency spectrum within which signals can pass without significant attenuation.

**baseline rule** - A ruled line positioned on the baseline of a piece of artwork, or at the bottom of a *computer screen*.

**BASIC** - Beginner's All-purpose Symbolic Instruction Code. A high level, widely used, *computer programming language* using basic English words, making it one of the easier programming languages for non-experts to use.

**batch processing** - A technique for *computer* operation in which *programs* and *their data*, or groups (*batches*) of data which have similar processing requirements, are processed individually, usually with one being completed before the next is started. This makes more efficient use of the *processors (CPUs)* of computers, particularly so for the many data calculations required for computer graphics processing. *Batch processing* is the opposite of *interactive processing*.

**Baud** - A rate-of-speed measurement used in the transmission of *data*, such as *computers* transmitting data over telephone lines through the use of *modems*. Divide the quoted *baud* rate by the number of *bits* required per character to derive the transfer-rate-per-second. To roughly translate into characters, divide by 10, ie: 1,200 baud is 120 characters per second.

**BBOP** - A three-dimensional, key-frame based, *computer animation* system developed by G Stern in 1983, at *NYIT*.

**BCS** - British Computer Society.

**beam position** - The location on the *CRT screen* which is being excited, and therefore illuminated, by the electron beam.

**beam splitter** - A mirror system that enables a camera-person to film, or record, two images simultaneously from the same point of view.

**beam spot size** - The diameter of the illumination caused by the *CRT's* electron beam at the point where it touches, or shines on, the *CRT screen*.

**BEFLIX** - A *language* developed by Ken Knowlton in 1964, which was used to produce some of the early *computer animation* films.

**behaviourial animation** - In behaviourial *animation*, rules are defined to govern the actions of certain classes of objects in the system. The rules interact with one another to create behaviour that is somewhat, but not totally, predictable. A common example is fish - they swim within specific speed parameters, turn within a certain turning radius, avoid solid objects and have an inbred urge to stay near the center of the school.

**bells & whistles** - Those little add-ons, or "fringe benefits", to a *system* or *software* package which do not really affect the basic performance of the system.

**benchmark** - A *program* used to assess the performance of a *computer*, particularly in terms of speed and precision. The performance is usually measured relative to other computers running the same program.

**bicubic Bezier patches** - A specific type of *bicubic patch* which blends well at boundaries with adjacent patches. Developed by Pierre Bezier.

**bicubic interpolation** - The use of two cubic functions to generate interpolated values along a geometric surface. Cubic functions are more accurate than linear functions, and more difficult to compute, but yield superior results. The *algorithms* used in *bicubic interpolation* allow for a smoother, more accurate stretching of an image than through the relocation of *pixels*.

**bicubic patches** - A mathematical technique for the description of a curved surface in which two cubic functions are used in the representation. Such patches have more degrees of freedom (they can curve more) than *polygons*. *Bicubic patches* are therefore particularly adept at modeling smooth, rounded shapes. Today's bicubic patch is the result of several various refinements on the original parametric, bivariate cubic surface patch developed by Edwin Catmull in 1974.

**bi-directional printer** - A printer that prints both left-to-right and right-to-left, allowing consecutive lines to be printed without the time-consuming process of having to have the *print head* return to the left-hand margin before printing each line. This process is controlled by the printer's built-in operating *software*.

**Big Blue** - A nickname for International Business Machines Corp (*IBM*), derived from its blue corporate logo.

**bilinear interpolation** - The use of two linear functions to generate interpolated values along a geometric surface. Linear functions are simple and quick to compute, but often cause undesirable results.

**binary arithmetic** - A method of calculation which is relatively fast and simple. Numbers are represented as sequences of *binary* digits (0 or 1) rather than sequences of decimal digits (0 to 9), allowing computing machinery to represent numbers with only two possibilities for every digit.

**binary code** - A code for describing information that uses only two distinct characters, usually 1 and 0, or on and off. These are combined in various sequences to represent letters, numbers and symbols. Used mainly in *digital* computing. See also, *machine language*.

**binary coded decimal (BCD)** - A system of *binary* numbering in which each decimal digit is represented by four *bits*. (Telex uses a 6-bit code, IBM's EBCDIC is an 8-bit code).

**binary *n*-cube** - A generalized concept for terms in the geometric series *point, line*, square, *cube, hypercube*... which has become a well-accepted way of organizing *computers* with multiple *processors*. *Binary* means two processors share every edge.

**binary numbers** - Numbers which are represented by sequences of the two *binary* digits, 0 and 1.

**BIOS** - Basic Input Output System. The basic operating system for a *personal computer (PC)*, usually contained in a *ROM chip* and permanently installed in the computer's *hardware*.

**bipacking** - An in-camera, or in-optical-printer, *matting* process in which one image on already processed film is *composited*, or laid onto another un-exposed film without overlapping. A *bipac* of two unexposed films is occasionally used in the *Blue Screen* process.

**BIRA/IBRA** - Belgisch Institut voor Regeltechniek & Automatisering - Institut Belge de Regulation et d'Automatisation.

**bit** - A contraction of "binary digit". The basic unit of electronic information in a *digital computer*, a *binary* digit (*bit*) has the value of 1 or 0. The memory capacity of a computer is measured in terms of *bits*.

**bitblt** - Binary, or bit-wise, block transfer. An operation to move or exchange *bitmaps* at high speed while applying logical operations to either the existing, or new, contents of the bitmap, or between both. Commonly used to display temporary windows over an image and usually performed by a special hardware device called a *blitter*. See also, *pixblt*.

**bitmap** - When each *pixel* is controlled by a single *bit* of computer memory. This gives the graphics/animation program speed and flexibility, but requires a large computer memory to be used effectively.

**bitplane** - A two-dimensional storage area, one *bit* deep. *Frame buffers*, or *frame stores*, consist of one, or more, *bitplanes*.

**bit rate** - The speed at which *bits* are transmitted, usually expressed in "bits per second".

**blanking** - The time during which the electron beam of a *CRT* monitor is turned off and reset to its start position for either the next *scan line* or the next field.

**blitter** - See *bitblt*.

**block** - A group of words, characters or digits that is handled as a single unit, eg: moving a *block* of copy in a *word processing* document.

**block-structured syntax** - A characteristic of a *programming* language which allows the nesting of processes, or blocks of code.

**blooming** - A video phenomenon whereby streaks fan out into the image around an area of intense illumination.

**blue screen** - A filming technique in which a subject (actor, group of actors, other object) is photographed against a uniform blue background to simultaneously produce an optical *matte* as well as a color negative. In video production the blue background facilitates the *compositing* of separately filmed images into one scene.

**blueprint style** - A visual style using line drawings to produce either 2-D or 3-D *wireframe* images and models. Most often used to show the structural, or internal, make-up of an object. The name is derived from an older method used to reproduce architectural and engineering drawings, originally drawn on special linen fibre paper, and copied onto light sensitive, chemically set paper which produced white lines on a blue background.

**blurring** - A technique used to model objects so they present the idea of motion to the viewing eye. See *motion blur, aliasing*.

**board(s)** - See *circuit board*.

**body text** - The type used for the body of copy, or the main text, of a document. Usually 12 *points* or less in size, and distinguished from headings, captions and display lettering.

**boilerplate** - A *word processing* term that refers to a large, standardized block of text, it can also be used to refer to any standardized block of *data*.

**Boolean** - Pertaining to the symbolic logic system developed by British mathematician George Boole, containing an algebra of "and", "or", "not" and "exclusive or" operators.

**boot/booting/bootstrap** - A term for loading a *program*, usually the *operating system*, into a *computer*.

**BOPS** - billion operations per second.

**border** - A hard or soft line around a *character*, or any image, that may be keyed into a screen picture.

**Bosch FGS-4000/4500** - Three dimensional computer animation system, originally produced and marketed by Robert Bosch Corporation, and now by *BTS*. One of the first 3-D *systems* that was widely marketed, it found extensive use in broadcast, and video post production.

**bounding box** - A relatively simple object, usually a rectangle or box with the overall dimensions, or *bounds*, of a more complex object, that is used in place of that exact, more complex, modeled shape to represent an object in an animation preview, or to predict the inclusion of that object in the scene. This reduces the calculation/production time and expense when previewing *computer animation* sequences to check continuity, positions and timing.

**broadcast** - A one-way form of communications, usually going from one originating source to many receivers.

**brush** - Art media (paint, crayon, chalk) simulation for free-hand drawing on a *paint* system. Usually performed using a *stylus* and *digitizing tablet*, but a *mouse* or *keyboard cursor* keys can also be used. Brushes may vary in width, texture, shape and transparency.

**b-spline** - A technique for representing a curved surface using continuous or complex curves without having to enter a great many data points. Instead, the *b-spline* algorithm uses a small number of control points along the curve to define its shape.

**BTS** - Broadcast Television Systems Inc.  A joint company of Bosch and Philips that now markets the FGS-4500 and *EPIC*.

**bubble memory** - A type of *computer data storage* in which information is placed in a thin film of magnetic material in the form of bubbles.

**buffer** - An intermediate *storage* device, or storage area, for temporarily holding *data* that is being transferred between elements of a *computer system*, or between systems.  It can be either an area of the computer's *memory*, a separate memory area, a *magnetic tape* or a magnetic or *optical disc*.  In traditional *animation*, the term is also used to mean acceleration from rest to a given speed, or deceleration to rest from a given speed, similar to *ease* and *fairing*, when applied to pans and zooms.

**bug (debug)** - A problem or mistake, usually in the *software*.  Debugging is the process of correcting it.  The term dates from the earliest days of computers when their vacuum tubes attracted insects that caused short circuits.

**bullet** - A large dot used in typesetting, usually to emphasize points in lists or blocks of copy, or to mark dimensions of a page or layout.

**bump mapping** - A technique for simulating rough or physical textures on surfaces, by *perturbating* the surface normal during *Phong* shading.  See, *mapping*.

**business graphics** - The use of graphic representations, such as pie charts, bar charts and graphs, to show, explain and compare various aspects of business operations, historical performance and projections, usually statistical in nature, and to graphically depict relevant or comparative data.  Can be either printed, or produced on various types of film and electronic media for projection.

**bus** - A circuit, or group of circuits, which provide a common electronic *data* transfer path within a *computer*, or between two or more *devices*, or between computers.

**byte** - A set of contiguous *binary bits*, usually eight (sometimes seven) which represent a character, symbol or operation.

**byte addressing** - The ability to read and write individual *bytes* into *computer memory*.  It allows more detailed manipulation of the contents of the computer memory than *word addressing*, but requires more *precision* in specifying the memory location, or *address*.

**Byte by Byte** - A company that supplies two- and three-dimensional computer animation software for use on *personal computers* and graphics *workstations*.

C++ - An extended version of *ANSI* Standard C that adds the constructs necessary for object-oriented *programming*. Invented by Bjarne Stroustrup at AT&T Bell Labs in the early 1980s.

**Cache memory** - A high speed *memory* used as a buffer between a *computer's CPU* and main memory. It is used to store instructions, or *data*.

**CAD/CAM** - Computer Aided Design/Computer Assisted Manufacturing.

**CAESAR** - Computer-Animated Episode-Using Single-Axis Rotation. An early analog *computer animation system*, with some *digital* control, invented by Lee Harrison in the mid 1970s as a further development of his *Scanimate* computer animation system, and produced by Computer Image Corporation.

**CAFE** - An early *computer animation* system, based on geometrical forms and the sequences of those forms, developed by J Nolan and L Yarbrough in 1969.

**CAMD** - Computer Aided Molecular Design.

**camera** - A device for capturing still or moving images, seen through a series of lenses, and recording them on photographic film, electronic media such as videotape, or through the use of a *digitizer*, directly into a *computer's memory* as digitally encoded *data*.

**camera view points** - The direction from which a three-dimensional object, or scene, created in an *animation computer,* will be viewed or recorded. Most *computer animation programs* now have the capability of selecting one or more *camera view points*, with variable fields of view, which can be moved, or selected at will, by the operator/*animator*.

**CAMP** - An early *language* for the *computer-assisted* production of *animated* films, developed by J Citron and John Whitney Sr in 1968.

**cancel** - To back-out of an operation without performing, or recording any action.

**candela (cd)** - A measurement of light. The intensity of a point source that generates one *lumen* per steradian. Also called candle power.

**cap height** - The height of a capital letter from the *baseline*.

**capping** - A process that defines new surfaces where a clipping plane cuts through an object, ie: *capping* the cut portion of the object so it appears whole again. See also, *clipping*.

**caption** - A title or subtitle identifying what is on the *screen*.

**Cartesian coordinates** - A coordinate system that represents a two-dimensional plane by defining two perpendicular axis that meet at right angles at an origin point. By convention, the horizontal axis is the x axis, the vertical axis is the y axis. Each axis has a scale starting from the point of origin, which is used to describe the coordinate of any point by defining its x and y location. Devised by the French mathematician Rene Descartes (1596-1650).

**cartographic data base (CDB)** - *Data* which contains in digital form the x and y coordinates defining a geographical area.

**cartoon** - An animated film, usually with various *characters* and a set story line.

**CASE** - Computer Aided Software Engineering.

**cathode ray tube (CRT)** - An evacuated glass tube in which a beam of electrons is emitted and focused onto a phosphor-coated surface to create images, eg: a television set, a *computer monitor*.

**CAT, CT** - Computer Axial Tomography, *Computer Tomography*.

**CATV** - Cable television. The distribution of television broadcast signals directly to receivers over communications lines, usually dedicated to the purpose. Most *CATV* systems are paid subscription systems operated by commercial carriers.

**CCD** - Charge Coupled Device. A monolithic silicon structure in which discrete packets of charge are transported from position to position by sequential clocking of an array of gates.

**CCIR** - Consultative Committee, International Radio. International standard for composite *monochrome* video signals.

**CCITT** - International Telegraph and Telephone Consultative Committee.

**CD-ROM** - Compact Disk - Read Only Memory. Also called *optical disc*. Closely related to CD audio discs, the information on *CD-ROM* discs is stored in *digital* form as a series of microscopic pits and lands (flat spaces). These pits and lands (collectively called bumps) are moulded, or etched into the plastic surface of the disc, and are read by a *laser* beam which illuminates the surface of the bumps and translates them into *binary data*. A single 4.7 inch *CD-ROM disc* can hold over 600 *megabytes* of information (the equivalent of 1500 floppy discs). Originally only available as *WORM* devices, erasable, re-writable optical discs for general use were introduced late in 1988.

**cel** - In traditional *cel animation*, a sheet of transparent plastic, originally celluloid, hence the name, on which cartoon characters and other animated objects are drawn and/or painted. The *cel* is punched with registration holes on one side to ensure consistent positioning, and is transparent so it can be placed over, or under, other cels allowing characters to be placed over static backgrounds, or two subjects to be moved separately as each frame is filmed. In *computer animation*, *cel* refers to a single-frame image.

**cel animation** - Animation produced by means of recording sequential *cels*, one for each frame, or for every two frames, as opposed to mechanical movements performed on the *animation stand*, or hand animation of cutouts and flat models under the camera. *Computers* are now being used to produce the outline drawings for the cels, and the *in-between* movements from frame-to-frame, the outlines then being hand colored and finished. Also referred to as frame-by-frame animation.

**cel punch** - A punch designed to punch registration holes in *cels*, or paper for *backgrounds*.

**cell** - An object built out of *polygons* and recorded in a display list.

**centered** - Text or graphic elements placed in the middle of a line with equal distance from the right and left margins.

**central processing unit (CPU)** - The main processing section of a *computer*. The *CPU* is the manager of the system resource, its operation controlled by a list of instructions. It can also contain the arithmetic-logical unit, registers, etc.

**CFD** - Computational Fluid Dynamics.

**CGA** - Computer Graphics Adapter. An early graphics display standard for *IBM* compatible *personal computers*. Replaced by *EGA*.

**CGI** - Computer Generated Imagery. Or, Computer Graphics Interface.

**CGL** - Computer Graphics Lab, usually referring to the *CGL* of *NYIT*.

**CGM** - Computer Graphics Metafile. An international standard for describing *computer graphics* images so they can be communicated between different *systems* without error or ambiguity.

**chain printer** - A *computer* operated *device* that prints at high speed on a continuous length of paper, using individual *characters* mounted on an endless (looped) chain. As the proper character rotates to the point of impact, it is struck onto the paper.

**Chameleon** - Low cost paint system made by Chyron.

**Chap** - The proprietary **Channel** Processor used in Pixar Image Computers which uses four computational elements to directly process data described for *RGB* and *Alpha channels* in parallel.

**character** - In *animation*, any person or animal who plays a part in an animated film (see *toon*). Also, a letter of the alphabet, upper or lower case, digit or special symbol.

**character compensation** - Reduction of the width value of each type *character*, thereby reducing the white space between characters for tighter fit. Also called *kerning*.

**character generation** - The construction or "drawing" of typographic images, or *characters*, on the face of a *CRT* by a moving electronic beam.

**character generator** - *Software*, or a complete *system* comprised of both *software* and *hardware*, which takes *character* data and causes corresponding character images to be created and appear on the *monitor* screen.

**character set** - The style of type chosen for output by the *printer*, also known as *type font*, or fount (UK). Some printers have very limited type or *character sets*, others, particularly *laser printers*, have the capability to print almost any font, providing that it has been described in a suitable *data* format.

**checker** - A *program* which can scan another program to see if it is grammatically correct. A *checker* allows one to catch errors early in the process of developing *applications* programs, when they are less time-consuming and less expensive to correct. A spell checker is a *checker* which catches word spelling errors in a *word processing* program.

**checkpoint disk** - A protective storage *device* which takes a "snapshot", or *checkpoint* record, of the contents of a *computer* periodically, so that one can recover from a computer failure by referring to the most recent snapshot, or checkpoint.

**CHI** - Computer Human Interface.

**chiaroscuro** - Shading.

**chip** - A very small piece of silicon, or more recently *gallinium arsenide*, upon which is etched an *integrated circuit* (IC), produced as an individual, self contained unit usually composed of thousands of logic elements, or millions of individual electronic components. *Chips* can be designed to perform specific tasks, ie: *processor chips, memory chips* (a "4K" memory chip stores 4,096 bits, a "64K" memory chip stores 65536 bits). *LSI, VLSI,* and *ULSI* are chips with very high numbers of circuits or *devices* per chip.

**choose** - To pick a *menu* item. You normally *choose* menu items with the menu button on a *mouse*, or with the *keyboard cursor* key.

**chroma** - A subjective term which usually refers to the difference of a hue from a grey of the same value. In a subtractive system, adding the complement will make the color darker. In an additive system, adding the complement will make the color lighter

**chromakeying** - The replacement of a single color signal (usually blue) with new visual information in a video image. See *keying*, *blue screen*, and *compositing*.

**chrominance** - A television/video term, indicates the hue and saturation of a color, or the color information without the brightness.

**chrome map** - An airbrush chrome simulation. See, *mapping*.

**Chyron** - Makers of a family of character generator equipment.

**CIE** - Commission Internationale Eclairage.

**cinex** - A test to determine the optimum exposure for the desired brightness and color quality of the filmed image.

**CIPS** - Canadian Information Processing Society.

**circuit board** - A flat, relatively thin, board of non-conductive material, onto which are mounted various electrical components such as *ICs*, resistors etc, all connected by circuits, most of which are etched into the board itself, together with various input and output connectors (plugs and sockets). One, or more, boards are usually assembled together to form a *computer*. A *personal computer* is usually made up of one *motherboard*, and several control, processor and/or memory boards. *Boards* communicate via a *bus* which is often contained on the motherboard. *Peripheral devices* also usually contain various *circuit boards*.

**classification** - The process of determining the percentages of each material present in a volume being studied, ie: such as in a component made of steel, aluminum and ceramic.

**clay animation** - Animation of three-dimensional figures or other objects made of clay, plasticine or other malleable material.

**click** - To press and release a *mouse* button.

**clipping** - The process of removing portions of an image which are outside the field of view, outside the boundaries of the display screen, or to slice objects into pieces. In effect, slicing an object into two, or more, parts as if with a knife. A *bounding box* allows a simple check to find if an object is inside, outside, or crosses the boundary (and if so requires *clipping*) of the scene. See also, *capping*.

**clock cycle** - The smallest period of time in a *computer* for which synchronized events occur, controlled by the computer's clock. Because of the disparity among computers as to how much work is done in a single *clock cycle*, it is a poor indicator of actual, or comparative computer speed.

**closely-coupled** - Referring to devices which take relatively little time to communicate with one another.

**closely-packed vectors (CPV)** - The technique of drawing a series of parallel lines from one side of a polygon to the other, which gives that polygon the visual effect of having a surface.

**cloud tank** - A water filled tank into which certain controlled chemicals and other substances are added to create cloud effects. A technique most commonly used for film *backgrounds* and special effects.

**CMY/(CYM)** - Cyan, Magenta and Yellow. The three basic colors of color graphic printing. See *YMCK*.

**coarse-grained** - Referring to parallel computing systems where entire *programs* or large *routines* execute concurrently on different *processors*.

**coaxial cable (coax)** - An insulated, central conducting wire, wrapped in another cylindrical conductive wire, and enclosed in a protective cable, designed to provide "*noise* free" signal transmission. *Coax* can carry large amounts of information, and is used to connect *computer terminals* and/or *workstations* to each other, and to their *host computer* or server.

**COBOL** - Common Business Oriented Language. A high-level *computer programming* language designed primarily for business or commercial use.

**code** - A symbol, or more usually a set of symbols, used to represent *data* or instructions to a *computer*. Also the actual writing of source instructions (*source code*) to be translated to machine instructions.

**coherence** - Commonly used in *raster* scan technology to describe the situation when two or more adjacent *pixels* share the same value. Raster graphics *algorithms* often make use of *coherence* to increase their efficiency.

**coke roll** - An outdated term for what is now described as *texture mapping*.

**collage** - A composition of flat objects, such as paper and cloth, pasted together on a surface and often combined with drawings and colors for artistic effect. A similar effect can be created with *computers* using images input via a *frame grabber* or a *digitizer*. The combination of graphics and/or effects; or producing images with a mixture of media and textures, typography and/or photography.

**color** - The subjective interpretation of the *hue, value* and *chroma* of an object or image.

**color bar** - The set of colors available for use in an *animation* or *paint program*, displayed as a bar. See *palette*.

**color bars** - A standard set of colored areas, usually in the shape of bars, used in video recording for adjusting color values on a video *monitor*.

**color correction** - The process of adjusting color balances within an image prior to printing or display.

**color cycling** - A limited *animation* effect that presents (or repeats) the same frame, but with a different, or changing, color *palette*.

**color display** - A system, such as a *CRT*, which can display in more than one *color*. Usually refers to an *RGB* based full-color display.

**color map** - A table storing the definition of red, green and blue *(RGB)* components of colors to be displayed. See also, *lookup table*.

**color separation** - The process of separating the colors in a colored image (eg: a photograph or painting) into their primary colors (*YMCK* or *RGB*) for the purpose of reproduction by graphic printing or other methods.

**color space** - A three-dimensional coordinated system that defines colors organized in space by attributes such as *hue, saturation* and *value* (HSV), or red, green and blue *(RGB)*. A physical model of a color space is called a color solid.

**color table** - See *color map*.

**color table animation** - Creation of an *animation* effect by a predetermined changing of colors over selected portions of the scene.

**color test** - Also known as a *"wedge"*. Usually one or more frames of a production, or individual scenes in that production, rendered in full color, which accompany the *pencil test* so that colors in scenes can be judged along with motion and timing. This is a much more economical, and faster, procedure than rendering all the frames in the complete production.

**COMDEX** - Computer Dealer's Exposition. A major, annual, computer equipment exposition in the USA.

**command** - A *code* or set of instructions that can be keyboarded, or selected from a *menu* list or *icon*, and entered into a *computer's* memory, that will instruct the computer, and/or any *device* it controls, concerning the operations to be performed.

**command language interpreter** - An interactive system that invokes a collection of standardized prompts with a consistent syntax. Widely used in *computer* graphics systems. *BASIC* is usually an interpreted *language*.

**commentary** - The narration or spoken description in a film or video. Particularly in documentary and instructional films, or other films without dialogue.

**commentator** - An actor or spokesperson who speaks a *commentary*.

**commercial** - A film or video advertising or promoting a product or service, particularly for broadcast on television, although versions are also used in film theatres.

**communication link** - A fixed connection between two *processors* for the exchange of *data*.

**compiler** - A *program* that converts, or translates, English-like commands into instructions that can be executed by a *computer*. Unlike a *command language interpreter*, this is not *interactive*. *FORTRAN* is a compiled *language*.

**complementary colors** - Pairs of colors opposite each other on the *hue circle*. In an additive system, complementary colors combine to produce white. In a subtractive system, complementary colors combine to produce black. When *complementary colors* are placed adjacent to each other, they produce vibrant effects typical of "optical art".

**complex numbers, complex arithmetic** - Numbers which represent points on a plane, just as ordinary numbers can represent points on a line. They require twice as much *storage*, and many times as much arithmetic, as ordinary numbers. *Complex numbers* arise throughout higher-level mathematics and are essential for many kinds of scientific *simulation* and signal processing tasks.

**composite shot** - Any combination of different images into one image. A film or video picture or sequence that combines two or more original scenes by means of *mattes*, split screen, back projection or other techniques.

**compositing** - The process of merging several partial or whole images to produce one complete final image. In *computer animation* it is frequently necessary, or more convenient, to generate the various elements of a picture separately and merge them together afterwards.

**composition** - The total process of combining various elements, components or images into one whole image. The assembling of images, photos, illustrations and type so that all elements are correctly positioned, according to aesthetic and ergonomic criteria, on the *computer monitor* or printed page.

**compute** - To manipulate an amount of numbers, to ascertain information by calculation.

**computed tomography (CT Scan)** - A medical, radiographic, diagnostic technique that creates a series of cross-sectional views of an object (such as a human body) by passing X-rays through it from many different angles. Using special *computer animation programs*, a series of the resulting images can be used as input to generate three-dimensional views of the object.

**computer** - A device capable of producing useful information or functioning by accepting *data* and processing that data and performing prescribed operations. Usually a machine equipped with *keyboards*, electrical circuits, electronic *devices*, storage devices, *output* and recording devices that processes information/data and performs mathematical and logical operations at high speed. An information processor.

**computer animation** - *Animation* produced with the use of a *software program* and a *computer* to draw or model each frame, produce the *in-betweens* and color them, as opposed to animation produced with *cels*, *clay*, or *puppets* etc.

**computer assisted animation** - Using a *computer* to assist, or facilitate, the production of traditional style, basically hand drawn, *animation*. See *scan and paint*.

**computer-controlled animation** - *Animation* produced by using a *computer* to control the movements of an *animation stand* or *motion control* camera. Makes possible a greater degree of accuracy, repeatlability, sophistication and speed of operation.

**computer-generated animation** - *Animation* produced using a *computer* and various *software programs* to create images within the computer and manipulate them. These images exist as digital information until they are *output* to the *CRT monitor*, film/video recorder or printer.

**computer graphics** - The overall discipline of creating, or manipulating, graphic images and pictorial data with *computers*. These can be used for *CAD*, *animation*, design, architecture, scientific imaging, *business graphics*, etc. *Computer graphics* systems are usually *interactive*, displaying the images on a computer *screen* as they are being created or manipulated.

**computer instruction** - An instruction, either in *source code*, or *machine language*, directing the *computer* to perform some operation specified by the instruction.

**computer output microfilm (COM)** - A *device* for recording images displayed on a *CRT*, composed of a camera equipped with various color filters, housed in a light-tight box, pointed at a high-resolution CRT. The camera is driven directly by the *computer*, and the exposure time depends on the number of *vectors* to be drawn.

**computer program** - A set of instructions which, when converted to machine-readable format, causes a *computer* to perform a series of specified operations to achieve the desired end result.

**computer vision** - Technology concerned with the perception of images and identifying objects. Used to read bar-codes, recognize faces, inspect manufactured parts. *Computer vision* technology operates by converting *pixels* into lines and shapes, and then determining what those images represent or relate to, usually specific *data* in *memory*. This is now considered a discipline of *artificial intelligence (AI)*.

**concatenate** - To link together as in a chain, one after the other.

**condensed** - A typeface in which the width is proportionally less that its height, thereby occupying less linear space that standard type.

**configuration** - The way in which the components of a *computer* and its *peripherals* are linked and programmed to operate as a *system*.

**conic generator** - A function generator capable of drawing any conic section, ie: any parabola, hyperbola or ellipse.

**continuity** - The matching of action and content in a film or video so that they appear to represent a real or imaginary world, and appear in logical sequence. In *computer graphics*, the matching and aligning of sub-surfaces (typically patches) so that they form a continuous surface.

**continuous shading** - A smoothly varying shaded surface, produced by using intensity, or surface, interpolation methods.

**contour characters** - Letters having a continuous, even-weight line drawn around the outside of the character, but not touching it.

**contrast** - the ratio of the brightness of an image to its surrounding background.

**control store memory** - Memory within a *computer* in which the microcode *program* is stored, in contrast with *memory* used to store *data*, images or high-level programs.

**control unit** - That part of a *processor* which determines what to do and when, based on instructions stored in *memory*.

**conversion (standards)** - See *standards conversion*.

**convolutions** - Filtering techniques used to sharpen (high-pass filtering), or soften (low-pass filtering) an image for purposes of image enhancement. Mathematical operations are performed on a group of *pixels*, in which each pixel surrounding the 'pixel of interest' is multiplied by a selected integer and summed to produce a result which replaces the original pixel of interest.

**coordinate** - One or several numerical quantities which between them serve to define the position of a point in a *coordinate* system, ie: on a plane, or in space.

**coordinate systems** - Systems by which the position of a point may be defined numerically. The commonest systems are *Cartesian coordinates* and *Polar coordinates*.

**coplanar** - A technique for building three-dimensional models from two-dimensional blueprints by using two coplanar views, a plan view and an elevation.

**copy** - A reproduction or imitation of an original. Also, manuscript type, the wording in a document, or the written portion of an assembled image.

**Core** - An early standard for three-dimensional graphics information interchange.

**core (storage)** - *Magnetic Core* Storage, an early type of *memory* storage which used magnetic *cores* as the storage medium. The term is now often used, incorrectly, to refer to the internal, semiconductor *memory* within a *computer*, as opposed to storage on *peripheral devices*.

**courseware** - Software written for educational purposes.

**CPI** - Characters per inch, a measure of *type* size or density.

**CP/M** - Control Program for Microprocessors. An early *disc operating system (DOS)* for micro *computers* developed by Digital Research Inc. Now largely superseded by *MS-DOS*.

**CPM** - Critical Path Method. An older *program* for project management.

**CPU** - *Central Processing Unit*. The *control unit* of a conventional, sequentially-organized *computer*.

**CPV** - *Closely-packed vectors*.

**crash** - What happens when a *computer* becomes inoperable because of *hardware* malfunction or *software* error. Derived from "head *crash*", when the read/write head of a *disk* drive touches the disk itself at high speed.

**crawl** - Text characters moving at an easily readable rate across the screen, usually horizontally or vertically.

**Cray** - Family of super computers manufactured by Cray Research Inc.

**credits** - The listing, in a series of titles, of the names and job functions of all the people and organizations who worked or contributed to that specific production.

**cross-dissolve** - See *dissolve*.

**cross-fade** - To blend slowly from one image to another. A common method of connecting two sequences in film/video editing. See *fade in/out*.

**cross-hair digitizer** - A hand held device fitted with a "cross-hair" target, which is used to *input* drawing data-points onto a *digitizing tablet/table*. The cross-hairs are positioned over the point to be input, and a button is pushed to register that point into the *computer's digital memory*. See *puck*.

**cross talk** - In telecommunications, the unwanted transfer of energy from one circuit to another.

**CSZ** - Computer Society of Zimbabwe.

**CT (scan)** - *Computed Tomography*.

**cube** - a six-planed, or six-sided object in three-dimensional screen space.

**Cubicomp** - Manufacturer of the *personal computer* based *PictureMaker*, and *workstation* based *Vertigo V2000* three-dimensional *computer animation* and modeling systems.

**cursor** - Any device which enables a point to be indicated. On a *CRT* or video display terminal it consists of a moveable symbol, normally a horizontal bar or vertical cross, often flashing, which can be positioned horizontally and vertically to indicate the point at which the next action instigated by the operator will take place, eg: where the next letter will appear on a *word processor*, or where a line will start, or the point around which it will bend, in a graphics display. *Paint* programs use *cursors* to show where the paint will be applied when the stylus is pressed down.

**cushioning** - See *fairing, ease*.

**cut and paste** - To copy, or move, a section of selected size or dimensions from one place on the *computer screen* to another, or from one computer file to another. Can apply to both text and graphics operations.

**Cyber** - Family of high-performance supercomputers manufactured by Control Data Corp.

**cycle** - An action designed to repeat itself after a certain number of *frames*, allowing the frames to be looped together, either physically or electronically, to extend that action without having to produce more original frames. eg: a walk *cycle* for an animated character.

**Cypher** - A *character generator* with three-dimensional capability manufactured by Quantel.

**CYM/(CMY)** - Cyan, Yellow and Magenta. The three basic colors of color graphic printing. The subtractive color primaries. See *RGB, YMCK.*

**DAC** - *Digital-to-analog converter.*

**daisy wheel** - A three-inch diameter metal or plastic flat wheel (disc) with typewriter characters on spokes radiating from its center. Installed in a printer or typewriter, the disc spins and as the keyboard is struck, a hammer strikes the disc from the rear to print the appropriate fully formed character onto the page.

**daisy wheel printer** - A printer that prints fully-formed characters through the use of a *daisy wheel.* Generally high quality, but relatively slow.

**DASD** - Direct Access Storage Device. A *device* such as a magnetic *disc* or drum that provides direct access to the *data* stored on it. As opposed to a *magnetic tape* drive that provides serial access.

**dash leaders** - Leaders, or space indicators, consisting of dashes (----). Generally used to facilitate visually lining-up text, columns and other material, separated by several spaces, on a line of type or on a *computer screen.*

**DAT** - Digital audio tape. Originally developed for the music recording industry, this technology is now being adapted for digitally recording *computer data*, mainly for use in tape back-up systems.

**data** - Facts, figures, or items of raw information, from which conclusions can be drawn, or which are used in various processes. See also, *discrete data.*

**data bank** - The mass storage of a large amount of information (*data*), indexed in a manner that facilitates selective placement and retrieval.

**database** - *Data* items that have been previously stored in order to meet specific information processing and retrieval needs. Generally refers to an organized collection of *records* stored in a *computer's memory.*

**Database Management System (DBMS)** - A *system* or *software program* which enables a *data base* to be created and organized to expedite the processing - storing, retrieving, sorting, and updating - of information, the generation of various reports, and the output of that information in specified formats.

**data communications** - The transfer or exchange of information between *digital* devices, such as *computers*, requiring the transmission of digital signals.

**data processing** - The storage, retrieval, manipulation and handling of *data.*

**data rate** - The rate at which *signals* can be transmitted.

**data reduction** - Extracting needed information from masses of raw *data* and organizing it into useful form. Can apply to any method for reducing the volume of data.

**data set** - A collection of *data*, a *file*. In some systems, the group of files that together outline the operations, handling and final format required for a specific data processing task.

**data structure** - The organization of a collection of similar *data*, or a group of related *records*, in a manner designed to preserve the relationships between various data, and facilitate its management and manipulation.

**data tablet** - A *computer* input device for encoding x-y information which is "drawn" or inscribed onto its surface, generally with a hand-held *stylus*. Used mainly for two-dimensional images and hand-written *data* input (See also, *digitizing tablet*).

**data transmission** - The sending of *coded* information, or *data* over telephone, or other, communication lines.

**DBMS** - *Data Base Management System.*

**DDA** - *Digital Differential Analyzer.*

**DDES** - Direct Digital Exchange Standards.

**debugging** - Removing errors in *computer software*. See also, *bug*.

**DEC** - Digital Equipment Corporation, makers of the PDP and VAX line of computers.

**definition** - The number of sensor cells (*pixels*) per line/column in a video display.

**deformation** - In *computer animation,* changes in the geometry of an object to give the illusion of creating action.

**demodulation** - The process of retrieving an original signal from a modulated carrier wave. One use for this technique is in *data transmission*, to make communications signals compatible with business machine signals.

**density (color)** - The relative *saturation* of an area with a color quality, ie: *chroma* or *hue*.

**density (film)** - The optical density of an image on transparent film media. Logarithmically related to the *opacity* of the film.

**density (storage media)** - The amount of information that can be stored on a storage medium (eg: tape or disk) in a given amount of space.

**depth cueing** - Varying the intensity of an image or object according to its depth in space from the viewer. This technique is used to give the viewer a sense of depth, or distance.

**descender** - That vertical portion of a lower case alphabetic character that extends below the *baseline* of the other characters, eg: "p" and "y".

**desktop computer animation** - The production of *computer animation* and graphics using a stand-alone *system*, generally based on a *personal computer (PC)* that fits on a desk top, configured with appropriate graphics and video boards, peripherals, and a *turn-key* animation/graphics *software* package. *Output* is usually recorded on videotape.

**desktop publishing** - The use of *personal computers*, *word processing* programs with two-dimensional graphics capabilities, graphics and *paint* programs, and *laser printers*, to typeset and layout material such as newsletters, magazines, presentation documents and books. The material can be either printed in quantity on the laser printer, or the high-quality laser printer output can be used as *mechanical* artwork for traditional high-volume printing methods.

**desktop video** - The use of a *personal computer (PC)* based *system* to capture images from video (videotape or television broadcast), and modify them by manipulating the image, adding titles/text, other images and graphics, and re-recording them onto videotape. See, *genlock*.

**developmental** - Describes those *computer animation* production facilities that *develop* their own software, which they run on a variety of *workstations* and *computers* ranging from *mainframe* to *graphics* superminicomputers. The opposite to *turn-key* facilities. In the earlier days of computer animation production, all facilities had to be *developmental* by necessity.

**device** - In computer terminology, used to describe a piece of equipment that forms part of a *computer system* or its *peripherals*.

**device independent** - *Software*, particularly graphics software, which is able to interface with various *computers* and graphics *peripherals* without requiring any special adjustments or revisions.

**device intelligent** - *Software* which is able to detect the capabilities of the *hardware* it is interfacing with, and thus lets the hardware do more work, performing only those necessary calculations and tasks that the hardware can not do.

**dialogue** - The speech of two or more actors in a film or video production, as opposed to the speech of a *commentator*. Also, the interaction, using set rules, between a user and a *computer* or other machine.

**diffusion filter** - Procedure for softening an image by averaging each *pixel* and its eight neighbours, then writing that average value back to the original pixel. Also known as a *low-pass filter*.

**digital** - *Data* in the form of discrete *binary* digits as opposed to *analog* continuous data.

**digital compositing** - Taking images from disparate sources (film, video, *computer* generated images, photographs), digitising them, and then combining them into one image. Being *digital* images, their *pixels* can be manipulated, defined and combined to insure a high-quality final image. Since digital data is extremely reliable, there is non of the *generation* loss which has traditionally limited these processes.

**digital computer** - A calculating machine that expresses all the variables and qualities of a problem in terms of discrete (*digital*) units.

**digital differential analyzer (DDA)** - An older term used to describe methods for drawing lines on visual display units, basically a *program* for the conversion of a line defined by its two end-points into *pixels*.

**digital display** - An electronic display system based on discrete points (*pixels*) of information. Digital displays vary according to the number of pixels per screen.

**digital-to-analog converter (DAC)** - Interface that converts *digital* signals used by a *computer* into continuous *analog* signals, such as those required to control the intensity of light produced along a *raster* scan on a video screen.

**Digital Video Effects (DVE)** - Devices that allow *raster* manipulation of an image (shrinking, positioning, rotations, door swings etc). DVE is a trademark of NEC Corporation. See also, *ADO*.

**digitization** - The conversion of an *analog* signal to a *digital* signal for *data* communications and manipulation.

**digitizer (3-D)** - A device which can scan a three-dimensional object and input that image into a *computer* in three-dimensional form by capturing its x, y, and z coordinates at pre-determined locations.

**digitizing scanner** - An input *peripheral* which scans existing two-dimensional *analog* graphic and printed images, and transfers that information into *digital data* which can be processed by a *computer*.

**digitizing table** - A large *digitizing tablet*.

**digitizing tablet** - A graphic input device in the form of an electronic drawing pad. Used to encode two-dimensional graphic information, usually from drawings or plans, by capturing x and y coordinates in *digital* form at desired intervals, generally with the use of a *mouse, puck*, or *stylus*.

**DIN** - Deutsche Industrie Norm. The West German National Standards Institution.

**directory** - A listing of each file in a *data base*, including what is in it and where it is stored.

**Direct Broadcast Satellite (DBS)** - A direct satellite signal fed from the supplier, via satellite, to microwave dish antennas at receiver's, or subscriber's locations.

**direct color** - Sometimes called full color. Uses a 24-bit *frame buffer* with three 8-bit planes, one each for the red, green, and blue components of each *pixel*. The number of colors that can be displayed at one time is only limited by the number of pixels in the frame.

**direct entry** - On-line input to a *computer* or *terminal* from a keyboard.

**Direct Memory Access (DMA)** - Allowing one *processor* to have direct access to another processor's *memory*, in order to maximize speed of operation.

**direct view storage tube (DVST)** - A *cathode ray tube (CRT)* whose surface will retain an image for an extended period of time. The display does not need to be refreshed because low level electron flood guns sustain the illumination of the phosphors activated by the directed beam.

**directed beam** - A *CRT* deflection technique in which the beam is used to trace the object on the screen.

**disc** - A flat circular plate with a surface on which *data* can be stored at random, or non-sequential locations, by various means, depending on the disc's surface. Flexible *floppy discs* (8", $5^1/_4$", $3^1/_2$") and *hard discs*, have magnetic surfaces which are magnetized selectively by a recording head. *Optical discs* have a surface which is written to and read by a *laser* beam.

**disc drive** - The system or device which writes and/or reads information to the disc, either magnetically or optically.

**disc operating system (DOS)** - A *computer program* responsible for the housekeeping and communications functions needed to get the *disc storage system* and main computing *(CPU)* unit to work together. *DOS* also manages the complete system and handles communications with other *peripheral devices*.

**disc pack** - A stacked group of magnetic discs, either fixed or removable, which offer the benefits of large *data storage* capacity as well as random access to the stored data.

**discrete cosine transforms (DCT)** - A method of compressing signals to increase speed for video telephony (videoconferencing).

**discrete data** - *Data* that occurs in distinct units.

**disk** - See *disc.*

**diskette** - Normally refers to a $5^1/_4$ inch floppy *disc.* It is also used more and more to refer to a $3^1/_2$ inch disc.

**display** - A volatile visual representation of a *computer's output* as on a *cathode ray tube (CRT).*

**display buffer** - Storage or *memory* that holds all the *data* required to generate an image on a *CRT.*

**display controller** - Hardware which accesses picture instructions and *data* and displays the resulting image on a *display monitor (CRT).*

**display element** - The various parts, such as a point or line segment, which constitute portions of an image produced on a *CRT.*

**display file** - A block of *memory (file)* used to store graphics display instructions and *data.*

**display list memory** - A specialized form of *computer memory* designed to store lists of numbers, and instructions, used in producing graphic images.

**dissolve (mix)** - A method of smoothly switching from one scene to the next, by the *dissolve* of one scene into the next, in a film or video. Accomplished by overlapping a *fade-in* of the new scene over a *fade-out* of the previous scene.

**distributed data processing** - A computing concept in which some or all processing, *programming* and control, along with *input* and *output*, are done on different machines connected electronically. Also referred to as *networking*, integrated office systems, and/or *connectivity.*

**dithering** - A technique for simulating a large variety of colors (eg: 16 million) when only a few (eg: 256) are available, by sacrificing spatial *resolution.* Also, a class of *algorithms* for *anti-aliasing* and extending the apparent *hue* or tonal range of a *display.* These techniques include: 1) by adding random amounts (or *noise*) to *pixel* values; 2) by applying a "dither matrix", or *low-pass filter*; 3) *halftoning.*

**DMA** - *Direct Memory Access.*

**documentation** - The permanent record of operating manuals, specifications and use-directions that accompany and explain *computer software* and *systems*.

**dolly in, dolly out** - To move the camera towards, or away from, the subject, or object being filmed, the camera move being done while the filming/recording is in progress.

**door swing** - The rotation of an image on any screen axis.

**Dore** - Dynamic Object Rendering Environment. High level modeling and rendering software supplied by Ardent Computer Corp.

**DOS** - Disk Operating System, as in *MS-DOS*.

**dot leaders** - Leaders, or space indicators, consisting of dots (....). Generally used to help visually line-up text, columns and other material, separated by several spaces, on a line of type or on a *computer* screen.

**dot matrix** - A method of printing whereby each character is composed of an array of dots, as opposed to fully formed characters. *Dot matrix* printers are particularly suitable for use with *computers* because of their high printing speed and ability to print graphic images. Color dot matrix printers use a limited variety of colored ribbons to print colored images.

**double buffering** - The technique of having one *frame* displayed as the next frame is being generated in a second *buffer*. Once the second image is created, the buffers swap in a single *refresh cycle*, displaying the second image, while a third image is being created in the empty first buffer.

**download** - To transfer *data, programs* and/or information from a remote location into a *computer*. Sending to the remote location is called *uploading*.

**DRAM** - *Dynamic Random Access Memory.*

**drop shadow** - An effect in which a detached shadow is cast behind a particular object, such as a logo or line of type, in 3-D space, to enhance the illusion of depth and solidity of the object. Also used as a 2-D typographic effect. A *drop-shadow* is not a true shadow. It is formed from the silhouette of the object to be shadowed itself, rather than from rays of light. The shape is colored darker and offset slightly to simulate true shadow.

**drum plotter/drum scanner** - Scanners and plotters that operate in much the same way as flat plotters and scanners, except that the material being scanned, or plotted onto, is mounted on a rotating drum rather than a flat surface.

**DTED** - Digital Terrain Elevation Data.

**dual-ported RAM** - Main *storage* in a *computer* with the unusual feature of having two independent gateways in or out. ie: one gateway, or *port*, can send instructions to the control *processor*, while the other *port* sends *data* to another processor, eg: a display processor generating a screen image.

**Dubner** - A family of *character generators*, *paint systems*, and 3-D modeling *computers* manufactured by Dubner Computer Systems Inc.

**dumb terminal** - A *terminal* with no independent processing capability of its own. It only works when connected to a *computer*. A *smart terminal*, by contrast, has some data processing capability. An *intelligent terminal* can be used for local processing without connection to a central unit.

**dummy** - A mock-up or other representation of the final form, or object, to be produced. Often used to refer to a printed form.

**duplex (full duplex)** - The ability of two *devices* to transmit simultaneously and separately along the same communications channel. *Half-duplex* designates the ability of devices to transmit in both directions, but not at the same time.

**DVI** - Digital Video Interactive technology. Integrated *digital* video, graphics and audio technology that compresses video and audio sequences so that they can be stored on *CD-ROM* and played back in *real time* on a *personal computer*.

**DVST** - *Direct View Storage Tube*.

**Dvorak keyboard** - A more efficient layout for the standard (*QWERTY*) *keyboard*, developed by August Dvorak in 1932. By placing the most frequently used characters in the center of the keyboard, the home row of the *Dvorak* layout is capable of nearly 4,000 different English word configurations, as opposed to 100 on the traditional QWERTY layout, offering a productivity increase of up to 80 percent. This makes it eminently suitable for *computer* use, but it still has yet to make appreciable inroads on the use of the long entrenched QWERTY layout.

**Dynamic RAM (static RAM)** - Dynamic random access memory requires periodic refreshing since the stored *data* tends to fade, or discharge. *Static RAM* retains data as long as electrical power is supplied.

**dynamic range** - A consequence of the number of *data bits* per *pixel* in a *bitmap*. One bit per pixel will give a range of two values (eg: black and white), eight bits per pixel will give 256 values. In general, "n" bits gives $2^n$ values.

**ease(s)** - A term used to describe the rate of change of velocity in an action, or the acceleration and deceleration of an object, in *computer animation*. Also known as *cushioning*. See *fairing(s)*.

**east/west** - The horizontal, or x, axis of movement.

**edge(s)** - The side(s) of a *polygon*.

**edge detection** - The use of image-processing techniques to define, or identify, area boundaries within an image. This allows areas on the *screen* to be defined by their perimeter.

**editor** - A program which allows a user to write text. The first step in creating any application for a *computer* is to type it in using an *editor*. A *word processor* is a sophisticated editor.

**effects track** - A sound track carrying sound effects only. There can be more than one in a film or video, which are *mixed* with the speech and music tracks to form the final sound track.

**EGA** - *Enhanced Graphics Adapter*.

**EISA** - *Extended Industry Standard Architecture*.

**electronic mail** - A general term for the electronic distribution of messages that can be read immediately, or stored for reception or reading at a later time.

**electronic publishing** - The rapid distribution of published material in electronic *data* format using *computers*, *modems* and communications lines. The recipient can store the *electronically published* material in computer *memory*, read it on a computer *screen*, or print it out from the computer locally.

**electronic voice mail** - An extension of *electronic mail* that operates in the same way, but with recorded voice messages instead of written messages.

**electrostatic printers/plotters** - A printing system that creates an image by first depositing it as a negative electrostatic charge onto the paper, then flowing positively charged toner (black or colored) onto the paper. The positive toner adheres to the negative characters and images on the paper, and is then fixed to the paper by heat treatment. A process similar to that used in Xerography, or plain-paper photocopying.

**em** - A typographic measure, the width of the capital M in a particular typeface, which therefore varies according to the typeface used. Since this measurement varies for different type sizes, it is useful for specifying dimensions that need to be in proportion to the type characters, ie: an *em* dash is the width of an M, *em* space is a fixed width blank space equal in size to the *em*.

**embedded compiler** - A built-in way to directly execute *programs* written in a high-level *language*. An *embedded compiler* eliminates the need of most *computers* to first translate high-level languages into low-level sequences of instructions before they can be run. See also, *interpreter*.

**embedded language** - Miniature *programming* environments within an application that permit the user to customize and extend the application beyond what its designers had anticipated.

**embossing** - The effect of letters being raised from their background.

**emulator** - A *device* or *program* that allows another device to operate as if it were something else. An *emulation* program permits a *computer* or printer to imitate another brand or type in its operation.

**en** - A typographic measure, the width of the capital letter N, in a particular typeface. See, *em*.

**Encore** - A digital effects device manufactured by Quantel. See also, *ADO*.

**end color** - One of two colors at either end of a range of colors.

**end user** - The user who ultimately receives *computer* service or information.

**Enhanced Graphics Adapter (EGA).** A graphics display standard used by *IBM* compatible desktop *personal computers*. *EGA* is an *IBM* trademark.

**EPIC** - Expandable Performance Image Computer. A high performance *computer* designed for the computation and manipulation of computer images, manufactured by *BTS*.

**ergonomics** - The science of adapting machines and furniture to people to increase efficiency, comfort, flexibility and operating ease.

**Ethernet** - A *local area network (LAN)* for computers and office equipment developed by Xerox Corporation.

**execute** - To perform the operation, or set of operations, indicated in a *program* instruction, or program.

**Ex Machina** - A *developmental computer animation* production company in France, formed from the merger of *Sogitec* and *TDI's* production department.

**expanded** - A typeface in which its width is proportionally greater than its height.

**expansion slots** - Spaces in *computers*, pre-wired with the necessary connections, where additional *circuit boards* may be added to the computer to enhance its operation or add capabilities and capacity.

**expert system** - A particular class of *artificial intelligence (AI)* systems which rely on heuristic rules to encode expert knowledge. *Expert systems* can match or exceed the performance of human experts in certain well defined applications.

**EXPLOR** - Explicitly Provided 2D Patterns, Local Neighbourhood Operations and Randomness. A *language* developed by Ken Knowlton in 1970, designed for scientific and artistic applications.

**Explore** - A three-dimensional *computer graphics* and *animation software* package for *personal computers* and *workstations*, produced by TDI Systemes *(Thomson Digital Images)*.

**exposure (exposure time)** - The measure of the amount of light reflected by an object or scene over a given period of time. Used as a reference for the amount of illumination and brightness required in film and video recording.

**Extended Industry Standard Architecture (EISA)** - A *bus* design supported by a group of *systems* and *peripherals* manufacturers and vendors in competition to *IBM's* proprietary *Micro Channel Architecture (MCA)*, as used in its PS/2 line of personal computers. *EISA* is designed to extend the compatibility of existing AT bus systems with new 32-bit datapath systems and peripherals.

**external memory** - A *device*, or series of devices, capable of storing information, that expands a *computer's* internal, or main, *memory*.

**extrusion** - A method for converting a two-dimensional image into a three-dimensional object by extending, or *extruding*, it along a third axis.

**facsimile transmission** - A system that transmits a representation of a document over a *telecommunications* link. Commonly referred to as *fax*.

**fade in/out** - A gradual transition from a normal, visible image to black (*fade out*), or from black to a normal image (*fade in*). Can also be a gradual transition from normal to white (*fade* to white). See also, *cross-fade*.

**fade up/down** - Same as *fade in/out*.

**Fairlight CVE** - Computer Video Instrument manufactured by Fairlight Instruments. A low-cost *paint* and *digital-effects computer*, designed for *real-time* manipulation of still or live video images.

**fairing(s)** - A term used to describe the graceful rate of change of velocity in an action, or the acceleration and deceleration of an object, in *computer animation*. Also known as *cushioning*. See also, *ease(s)*.

**family** - Referring to related *typefaces*, which are generally grouped in what is known as a *family*. ie: Helvetica, Helvetica Bold, Helvetica Italic, Helvetica Bold Italic all constitute a *family* of type.

**Fantastic Animation Machine** - The name of a *developmental computer animation* production company in New York City.

**fast Fourier transform (FFT)** - A mathematical *algorithm*, developed in 1960, used to analyze a *signal*, including a video signal, in terms of its frequency components. This allows *digital computers* to rapidly process images and signals.

**fault tolerance** - The ability to recover from errors with minimum penalty to the user.

**fax** - *Facsimile transmission*.

**FDDI** - Fiber Distributed Data Interchange.

**feature film** - A full length film (or video) for theatrical, television broadcast or rental use, generally of a minimum one hour's duration, produced using any one of, or a mixture of, production techniques, such as live action, *animation* etc.

**FGS 4000/4500** - See *Bosch FGS 4000/4500*.

**fibre optics** - The use of glass fibres of very small diameter to transmit information and *data* via light waves.

**field (data processing)** - The smallest unit of information in a *record*.

**field (video display)** - One of two portions of the screen in an interlaced scanning *display* system.

**field rate animation** - *Computer animation* that is produced on video having movement in each *field* vs each *frame*. ie: *NTSC* video is recorded at 30 frames-per-second, and each frame has two interlaced fields, hence a total of 60 fields-per-second. Showing movement in each *field* vs each *frame* will produce smoother apparent motion.

**field size** - The area covered by the camera in any particular condition.

**file** - A collection of similar *data*, or a unit of *computer* data, stored on a *disc* or tape, but not in *memory*.

**file maintenance** - Adding, changing and deleting *records* in a *database* to keep it up to date.

**file server** - A common term for the *software* and *hardware* that perform the storage, distribution and retrieval functions for shared files in a *local area network (LAN)*. The *file server* controls the network communications and the definition and sharing of network resources.

**fill** - A command used by a *paint system* or a *computer animation program* to color a designated portion of the *screen*, or an image on it, by converting the outline shape into a solid color image.

**filled** - Refers to objects in an *animation*. If they are *filled*, they appear as shaded solids.

**film** - The material on which photographs are normally recorded.

**film archive** - A library of films or videos of historical interest.

**film library** - A library or collection of films and/or videos from which they are distributed to various users.

**filmloop** - Presentation of a series of images on a computer display screen so that they appear to be moving in *real time*.

**film maker** - A person who makes films or videos, usually as a producer or director.

**filtering** - In *anti-aliasing*, the use of a weighting factor to *interpolate* the value of a *pixel* from the *polygons* intersecting it. *Filtering* techniques are used to solve *aliasing* problems. In *image processing*, a class of *algorithms* for analyzing, modifying and enhancing the contents of *frame stores* (eg: a *low-pass filter*). Also, the use of electronic *devices* to remove or dilute static from *telecommunications* lines, and static, spikes and power fluctuations from electrical power lines feeding *computers* and *peripheral devices*. Also, the use of color, density or polar filters on a camera lens.

**fine-grained** - *Parallel computing* which is efficient even at the level of individual operations or groups of operations.

**finite-element analysis (FEA)** - A sophisticated, computerized structural analysis technique. See *finite-element mesh*.

**finite-element mesh (FEM)** - A representation of a solid object, typically used to perform engineering analysis such as stress or thermodynamic analysis. The object is represented as a set of simple elements, such as boxes or wedges, connected together in a grid. The results of the analysis are computed at the *nodes*, or corners of the elements.

**firmware** - *Software* or a *program* permanently encoded inside a *chip*, or *ROM*, which remains intact even if power is lost. Many routine operations are encoded into a *computer* in this way, eg: a computer's *BIOS*.

**first generation computers** - First generation *computers* used vacuum tubes and magnetic tape storage. The second generation used transistors and magnetic discs. The third featured *integrated circuits*. Fourth generation computers are smaller again and feature *microprocessors*, *micro-chips* and *networks*. Fifth generation computers, still in the future, will incorporate *artificial intelligence (AI)*.

**first generation (copy or dub)** - The first copy or dub directly from the master, or original production recording or negative.

**fish eye** - A rounded image with exaggerated perspective that encompasses a very wide angle field - up to a 360 degree field. A *fish eye* lens is one that takes in a similar super-wide-angle field image.

**fixed space** - A blank type space of a fixed width, such as an *em*, an *en*, or a fixed character space.

**flare down** - A glow that resolves into a defined image, or that reduces and disappears from the *screen*.

**flare up** - An image that bursts into a glow, or a glow that grows and increases in size on the *screen*.

**flash frame** - A blank *frame* inserted in a film or video to create a subliminal *flash*. Usually used for a cut-point to a new scene.

**flat shading** - A shading technique in which facets of a *polygonal* model are *rendered* as a single color, based on their orientation to the light and to the viewer. Objects appear to have facets similar to those of a cut diamond. Note: *Lambert* flat shading ignores the viewer position. In *Phong* shading, the viewer position is used to calculate specular reflection, or highlight.

**flicker** - The pulsation of an image. Sudden light fluctuations on a *CRT screen* that occur if the display is not refreshed at a sufficiently high rate.

**flip(s)** - 90-degree and 180-degree rotations that re-orient the image and provide mirror views.

**floating-point arithmetic** - Arithmetic which allows the decimal point to "float" as needed to allow numbers to range from very small to very large. *Floating point arithmetic* is essential for *scientific computation*, but is expensive to build into *hardware*.

**floating-point numbers** - Denotes numbers of continuously varying quantities, and which have a decimal point.

**FLOP count** - The number of Floating-point **O**perations required for a task. Addition and multiplication, for example, each count as one operation.

**FLOPS** - Floating-point operations per second.

**flops (logo flops)** - A disparaging term used to refer to stylistically "clichéd" title animations. Also known as "flying logos".

**floppy disc** - A thin, flexible, circular plate whose surfaces are covered with magnetized material, enclosed within a protective cover, capable of storing magnetically encoded digitized information, and which can be easily inserted and removed from a *computer's disc drive*. *Floppy discs* generally come in three sizes, 8", $5^1/_4$" and $3^1/_2$", and their size has been decreasing while their storage capacity has been increasing. An inexpensive, portable form of *memory* storage.

**flow chart** - A diagrammatic representation of a *computer program* in which symbols represent logical subdivisions of the problem solved, and the order in which they are executed.

**flush left/flush right** - Type set even with the left or right margins of a page or column. See also, *justify*.

**flying spot scanner** - A device that employs a rapidly moving spot of light to scan an area. The intensity of the transmitted or reflected light is sensed by a photoelectric transducer and recorded electronically. This technique is used to make high quality video copies of filmed material.

**focusing** - Bringing an image formed by a lens into *focus* so it is more sharply defined. Sharpening the image on a *CRT*.

**folio** - A page number placed at the top of a page. If placed at the bottom of the page, the number is a "drop folio".

**font, fount** (UK) - A complete set of alphabetic and numeric characters (*type*) and symbols in a single *typeface*, weight and size. eg: 12-point Helvetica is a different *font* from 10-point Helvetica.

**Foonley F1** - A unique, custom built, *animation computer* which includes a film printer capable of very high 4000 x 6000 line resolution. It was originally built by *Triple I*, then bought by Omnibus, and subsequently acquired by Intergon Corporation.

**format** - The organization of printed, displayed or stored *data*.

**format conversion utilities** - *Programs* which translate between one way of representing *data*, and another. Because of the proliferation of incompatible formats representing data on various *computers*, *format conversion utilities* are sometimes needed to move *files* and information from one computer to another.

**FORTRAN** - Formula Translator. A high level *computer programming language* oriented toward mathematical operations.

**Four-D** - Descriptive term used by Silicon Graphics to identify its 4-D GT super-fast *workstations*. The fourth dimension refers to time.

**Fractal** - A term, coined by Benoit *Mandelbrot* in 1975, for defining certain types of geometry. *Fractals* are mathematical descriptions of irregular shapes that occur in nature (ie: trees, mountains, coastlines) that nevertheless have sufficient regularity to be programmed into a *computer* using simple *recursive* or *iterative* functions. An important concept is that images are self-similar at different magnifications. This branch of geometry can be used to describe many natural objects more efficiently than with plane and/or solid geometry. See also, *Mandelbrot*, *Mandelbrot Set*.

**frame** - One complete image displayed on the face of a *CRT*, or produced onto photographic film, or videotape, by a camera. A film frame represents 1/24th of a second, an *NTSC* video frame represents 1/30th of a second.

**frame buffer** - A dedicated *memory* area in a *computer*, or in a separate dedicated *device*, for temporary storage of *pixel* data to be displayed in one *frame* on a *CRT*. The "depth" of the *frame buffer* is determined by the number of *bits* stored for each pixel, which determines the dynamic range or number of colors, and intensities, which can be displayed. If ordinary *memory* is used as a frame buffer, it requires a video circuit to read and display it.

**frame-by-frame animation** - See *cel*.

**frame capture** - See *frame grab*.

**frame grab** - Input of a single *frame* of live video into a graphics processor.

**frame grabber** - A *device* that accepts video as a *computer input*, digitizes it, and stores the information in image *memory*, typically, a *frame buffer*.

**frame store** - Device used for short or long-term *digital* storage of a series of single video images so that they may be recalled for production use at a later time. See *frame buffer, scanline buffer*.

**frame store processor** - Image *memory* with an associated display processor tailored for image computing applications.

**freeze-frame** - To hold a *frame* on a monitor as long as desired. Usually in reference to *freezing*, or holding, one frame from an on-going or live video.

**front-end computer** - A *computer* which allocates tasks to another, usually larger, computer. eg: a Cray *supercomputer front-ended* by a *DEC* computer.

**front projection** - Projection onto an opaque *screen* from the front, as is the case in most movie theatres and with most video projectors. An image projected onto an opaque background screen for rephotography with foreground action between the screen and the camera.

**full animation** - *Animation* where there is one frame drawn, or produced by a *computer*, for every frame, or every other frame, of a film or video, to produce maximum smoothness of action in the sequence.

**full crossbar** - An interconnection *network* which directly connects everything to everything else. Although it minimizes the time to communicate, its cost grows dramatically with the number of *devices* being connected. It is also an impractical method of connecting large *multiprocessor* systems.

**full-duplex communication** - The use of two different sets of frequencies by the originating and answering stations, enabling communications to take place in both directions simultaneously.

**full-duplex modem** - Devices that transmit a character over communications lines without echoing it back to the sender. The echoing is done by the receiving station.

**full length film** - a *feature film*.

**fully formed characters** - When the character, or type, is formed all at once, ie: as with a *daisywheel* printer.

**function generator** - A *hardware* unit used to produce a specific result, eg: such as moving a *cursor*.

**function keys** - Keys on a *keyboard*, usually programmable by a user, which are used for invoking dedicated operations of functions, such as "save file".

**fusion** - The synthesis of live-action reality and special effects, graphics techniques or *computer animation*.

GaAs - *Gallium arsenide.*

**gallium arsenide (GaAs)** - A compound used for the manufacture of *computer chips*, touted as the future replacement for *silicon.*

**gamma correction** - A process that improves the video image by correcting for the non-linear brightness response of the color phosphors used in *CRT* monitors.

**gas plasma display** - A flat, relatively thin (as opposed to a *CRT*) *display* panel that is composed of a fine grid of wires suspended in a special gas plasma environment, sealed between two panels, one of which is the transparent screen. Electrical current applied selectively to the wire grid causes the gas to glow, forming characters and shapes on the screen, usually red on black. *Gas plasma* displays are rugged, have good contrast, and can show various shades of "grey". Used mainly in *portable* and *laptop computers.*

**gather-scatter** - A phrase referring to the need to collect or disperse *data* so that a *vector* computer can always deal with quantities that are organized in lists.

**gateway** - A point in a communications *network* that provides a link between two or more networks. An intelligent *device* that interconnects dissimilar networks by performing the necessary *protocol* conversions to allow communication between both environments.

**generation** - Successive copies of an original visual image or audio track. Copies or prints from the original film, negative, videotape, or audiotape are called *first generation*, the re-copied version is called *second generation*. The resolution, contrast and general quality of film, or analog video or audiotape reproductions, deteriorate with each successive copy, or "generation". *Digitally* encoded or recorded copies do not deteriorate with successive generations.

GENESYS - A picture-driven *computer animation* system developed in 1969 by Ronald Baecker.

**genlock** - A circuit or device that synchronizes internally generated video to an external video source. *Genlock* allows the input of video signals/images into a *computer* for manipulation, and their output to video.

**geometric transformation** - An operation that moves or positions an object in either two- or three-dimensional space. It consists of *translation* (or movement), *scaling*, and *rotation.*

**Geographic Information System (GIS)** - A general term referring to the technology for using *computers* for the production of topographic maps.

**GFLOPS** - *"FLOPS"* stands for Floating-Point **O**perations **P**er **S**econd, and "G" stands for *"Giga"*, the scientific prefix denoting one billion. Usually pronounced *"gigaflops"*. The fastest serial computers currently have peak performances near 1 GFLOPS. See also, *MFLOPS*.

**GI** - Gesellschaft fur Informatik, the West German computer society.

**giga** - The scientific prefix denoting one billion.

**gigaflops** - See *GFLOPS*.

**GIGO** - Garbage In, Garbage Out. Referring to the fact that current *computers* can only perform according to the level of their instructions and available *data*. Garbled or incorrect *input* results in garbled or incorrect *output*.

**gimbel** - To mount models or artwork in such a manner, usually by using a *motion control* device, that allows movement in multiple directions.

**GIS** - *Geographic Information System.*

**GKS/GKS-3D** - Graphical Kernal System, an early graphics standard, since updated to accommodate three-dimensional graphical images.

**glass shot** - A technique in which an image is added to a scene by positioning it on a clear glass plate that is larger than the camera's field of view, and photographing it together with the rest of the scene.

**glint** - A glimmer or sharp point of light. In traditional film work, usually created by *fading-up* or *fading-down* on a pinhole of light with a star filter or diffusion filter.

**glitch** - A *computer* oriented term referring to a small error in the execution of a *program*, or an unevenness in a graphics sequence.

**global operator** - A function that is applied to an entire picture, rather than to a subset. See also, *neighbourhood operator*, *point operator*.

**glow** - A mist, or soft edged halo of diffused light surrounding, or appearing to emanate from, an image.

**Gouraud shading** - A smooth shading routine that computes the color and illumination at each corner of a *polygon*, or on each side of a flat surface, and then interpolates these colors across the surfaces. Developed by Henri Gouraud in 1971.

**GPC** - *Graphics Performance Characterization.*

**graded series** - A scale of colors used in graphics to represent change in a variable. A graded series may be composed of progressive change in *saturation* of one *hue*, or along the grey scale.

**GRAFEDIT** - A graphics editor *program*, developed by a group under the direction of Nadia Magnenat-Thalman in 1981.

**graftal** - A type of procedural modeling that creates plants and trees by describing them in mathematical terms, using *algorithms* developed by Alvy Ray Smith (which he based ultimately on math by Lindenmayer).

**graphic display device** - A display *terminal* or *monitor* used to display data in graphic form. The most common type of *graphic displays* are *direct view storage tubes (DVST)*, *raster refresh* devices and *vector* (or vector stroke) refresh devices.

**graphic input device** - Device such as a *digitizing tablet* or *digitizing scanner*, which supplies the co-ordinates of graphic images, or type, in such a way that the image can be stored, reconstructed, displayed and manipulated by the *computer*.

**Graphical User Interface (GUI)** - The *interface* between a user and a *software program*, which determines the way in which the user accesses the program. It helps impart a visual, and tactile (eg: through *mouse* controls), "look and feel" to the program, which is an important element to the user's perceived satisfaction. Some efforts are being made within the software industry to standardise various graphical interface elements.

**graphic output device** - Device used to display or record an image generated on a *computer*. A display screen (*CRT*) is an output device for volatile *soft copy*; *hard copy output* devices produce permanent images on paper, film, videotape or transparencies.

**Graphics Performance Characterization (GPC)** - A new standard for measuring *display* and *workstation* graphics performance, being developed by *NCGA* with industry support.

**graphics preprocessor** - An extension of a *compiler* which permits the syntax of an existing *language* to be augmented by new graphics commands.

**graphics tablet** - An electronic drawing pad for graphic *input*. See *digitizing tablet*.

**graphics workstation** - A *workstation* with dedicated graphics *software* and *hardware*, which can therefore achieve a very high performance, and often real-time processing, of 3-D images, either in *wireframe* or solid shaded display modes.

**GRASS** - Graphics Symbiosis System. A user-oriented, real time, *computer animation* system developed by Tom DeFanti in 1972, at Ohio State University. The first computer animation system that was easily usable by "non-experts". See also, *ZGRASS*.

**grid** - A pattern of horizontal and vertical lines, usually at right-angles to each other. An internally generated (by a *computer*) pattern of intersecting lines which may be used to position images or be manipulated as part of the design. Sometimes used in *computer animation* as a background device to impart depth, or a technical look, to an image ("the dreaded green grid").

**GS-L-SM MTPS** - *Gouraud*-Shaded, Light-Source-Modeled Mesh Triangles Per Second. An attempt at defining some performance standards for graphics systems.

**GUI** - *Graphical User Interface.*

**gutter** - The white space between columns of type on a printed, or displayed, page.

**hairline** - A very fine or delicate line.

**half-duplex communication** - Enables telecommunication in only one direction at a time.

**half-duplex modem** - A *modem* which echoes back every character it transmits.

**halftoning** - A method for extending the apparent dynamic range of a *bitmap display* by using groups of *pixels* (eg: a 3 x 3 *array*) to represent single intensity values. Originally referred to as a kind of *dither* technique. See also, *dithering*.

**handshaking** - The synchronising of a transmitting *device* and a receiving device by the use of *software* or *hardware protocols*, or *handshaking* signals.

**hard copy** - A printed, tangible, non volatile copy of *data*, information or graphic images, such as a 35mm slide, or printed paper.

**hard copy device** - A device for producing *hard copy*, such as a *printer*, plotter, video or film recorder.

**hard disc** - A disc made of rigid ceramic-like material with a magnetic coating, and which is generally not removable from its drive housing. It stores much more *data* than a *floppy disc*. Often "stacked' into multi-disc assemblies providing very high, rapid access, data storage capacity.

**hardware** - The actual equipment which makes up a *computer system*, as opposed to the *(software) programming* or instruction sets for the system.

**hardwired** - *Program* or operating information "wired" or built into the *computer*.

**harness** - A term coined by Inmos Corp for the *language* construct that describes how multiple *programs* fit onto multiple *processors*. The *harness* not only describes which programs and *data* reside on each processor, but also how they are to be loaded and *harnessed* together.

**Harry** - A digital-disc video recorder, made by *Quantel*, which stores up to 84 seconds of *real time* video in single *frames* in a *random-access, hard disc* memory.

**head** - The electromagnetic device inside a *disc* drive that reads, records and erases *data* on the disc.

**hero shot** - A perfect take, or photographic sequence.

**heterogeneous database environments** - Distinct computing platforms upon which *database* software is designed and operated. Each of the three generally used current platforms, *microcomputer*, *minicomputer*, and *mainframe*, represents a different level of technology with its own methods of operation.

**Hexadecimal (hex)** - A *computer* system of counting that uses 16 numbers, or "base 16". A hex number can be represented by 4 *bits* ($2^4$), or a *nybble*.

**hidden line removal** - A process that uses *software* to remove or eliminate lines that would normally be hidden from view in the presentation of a wire-frame model. The result is a more realistic looking object. See also, *occultation*.

**hidden surface removal** - A software technique for rendering objects and scenes as solid surfaces. Parts of the scene that point away from the view position, or are occluded by nearer objects, must be determined and rejected. See also, *occultation*.

**high contrast** - Refers to films which eliminate to a large degree the intermediate values of the grey scale, resulting in an extremely defined black and white (or clear) image.

**high definition television (HDTV)** - A proposed television system with nominally twice the number of image *scan lines* (*NTSC*) as current television, ie: 1024 lines vs 512, giving a much sharper, higher *resolution*, picture. However, it has yet to be standardized, and the industry is far from a consensus, eg: the Sony system has 1125 lines.

**high-level language** - An English-like *language* whose statements must be *compiled*, or *interpreted*, into a *program* to be run on a *computer*. *BASIC*, *FORTRAN*, and C, are high-level languages.

**highlight** - A bright, small area in an image which contrasts sharply with the surrounding image. The reflection of a light source from the surface of an object, with the qualities of the *highlight* being determined by the qualities of the object's surface, and the position of the light source and of the viewer.

**high pass filter** - A *device* or *software* process that enhances high *spatial* frequencies or *attenuates* low spatial frequencies, in order to bring out detail in an image. See also, *sharpening filter*.

**high resolution** - A relative term that is used to describe any screen image produced with appreciably more than the *NTSC* standard 512 line video picture. Resolution is usually described in relative number of *scan lines*, (eg: 2000 line), or by *pixel* ratio (eg: 768 x 512), and a *high resolution* image generally refers to one with a minimum of 1000 lines.

**highly parallel computers** - A *computer* which uses 16 to 64,000 processors in "parallel". The processors divide, and independently work on, small portions of a large problem. Parallel computers excel at programs with many independent operations that can be done at the same time, and are particularly well suited for graphics work. They cost considerably less than *supercomputers*, although matching their speed. However, programming them can be difficult. See also, *Linda*.

**histogram** - A technique for displaying the count of *pixels* that share the same intensity value. Used in *image processing* and *image analysis*. Color images require one *histogram* for each primary color.

**HKCS** - Hong Kong Computer Society.

**HLL** - High level languages. High level *programming languages*, such as *COBOL* and *FORTRAN*.

**HLS** - *Hue-Luminance-Saturation*.

**homogeneous architecture** - A computer design which has communications, *processors*, and *memory* distributed evenly throughout it.

**HOOPS** - Hierarchical Object-Oriented Picture System. An emerging, highly portable, three-dimensional graphics standard.

**horizontal track camera** - Used in shooting (filming/recording) models, art (on a light box), matte painting, etc, where a *motion control camera* runs back and forth along a horizontal track, much like the action of a standard camera on a *dolly* track.

**host computer** - The central *computer* which provides computing power for *terminals*, *workstations*, and *peripheral devices* that are connected to it. See also, *file server*.

**host-satellite system** - A system relationship in which a satellite *computer* connects to another, usually larger, *host computer* for more extensive *data* manipulation or processing.

**hue** - Subjective term which refers to the objectively measurable dominant wavelength of radiant energy in the visible portion of the electromagnetic spectrum, the most basic attribute of color. Also, the angular coordinate in polar colorspace, such as *HLS*. Used loosely, *hue* can also be used to refer to mixtures of different wavelengths, such as purple.

**hue circle** - An arrangement of the color *hues* progressing from red through to blue, then violet, and back to red. Contains the many discrete and small color variations discernible to the human eye.

**hypercube** - A higher-dimensional analog of a cube. Just as a three-dimensional cube can be represented on a two-dimensional sheet of paper, a higher-dimensional cube can be conceptualized in three dimensions and used as the basis for a *multiprocessor computer* design.

**hyperspace** - An effect which is the result of visually streaking through a computer generated *star field*, to give the illusion of very-high-speed travel through outer space.

**IBM** - International Business Machines, the largest computer manufacturer.

**IBM compatible** - Refers to *personal computers* manufactured by a wide range of other manufacturers, which are very close copies of (clones), or which use the same *operating system* (*IBM-DOS*, *MS-DOS*) as IBM's line of personal computers. They therefore can use the same *programs*, and can exchange *data* with them, and among themselves.

**IBM-DOS** - *IBM's* version of *MS-DOS*.

**IC** - *Integrated Circuit*.

**ICARE** - *Interactive Computer-Aided RGB Editor*.

**icon** - A picture symbol. Used with some software and hardware systems to represent tools, commands and operations which can be selected by pointing at them with a *cursor* arrow, controlled with a *mouse*, or *stylus*. This type of user interface was developed at Xerox Park, and called *Smalltalk*. It was made popular by Apple Computer's *Macintosh* system.

**ICS** - Irish Computer Society.

**IDLS** - Image Display List System. Software developed by Visual Information Technologies.

**IFIP** - International Federation for Information Processing.

**IGES** - Initial Graphics Exchange Specification. A very popular method of moving data from one graphics system to another, developed in 1979.

**III** - *Information International Inc*. Also known as *Triple I*.

**Illusion** - A *digital* video effects device manufactured by Digital Services Corporation.

**image analysis** - The process of extracting useful information from images, such as estimating types of surface ground cover from satellite photographs.

**image averaging** - The averaging of a small area of an image to reduce picture resolution. See also, *pixellization*.

**image computing** - A term developed by Pixar to describe the capability of their image *computers* to provide both general-purpose *computer graphics* and *image processing* capabilities in a single system.

**image definition area** - A two or three dimensional space in which graphics images may be defined. Typically larger than the *screen*, the screen area represents a *window* into this area.

**image enhancement** - Techniques used to improve the quality of images by removing noise, or by bringing out, or enhancing, details that would otherwise be difficult to perceive.

**image mapping** - Taking a picture and applying it to, or stretching it around, a surface, particularly the surface of a *computer* generated object or three-dimensional model. The picture can be either a still photo or a *real-time* video image. See also, *texture mapping*.

**image memory (bit map)** - *Memory* which holds the *digital* representation of an image.

**image processing** - The capture and manipulation of an image in order to extract useful information from it, or to enhance the quality of that image. Using a *computer* to clarify, interpret, or manipulate a real or synthetic image. Images from satellites, and space probes, for example, require considerable processing before they can be converted into photographs.

**image repainting** - Adjusting or manipulating colors through optical or *computer* generated *rotoscoping* techniques.

**image space** - See *screen space, world space*.

**image synthesis** - The creation of two and three-dimensional images from mathematical models with the aid of *computers*.

**image understanding** - *Image processing* and *image synthesis* combined with *artificial intelligence*.

**image warping** - See *warping*.

**Images II** - A paint/graphics system developed by the New York Institute of Technology (*NYIT*) and manufactured by Computer Graphics Labs (*CGL*).

**Imax** - A large, 70mm film format which encompasses three standard *frames*, and requires a specially designed *camera* and *projector*.

**IMI** - Interactive Machines Inc, manufacturers of a family of *computer* image generation systems.

**impact print** - When printed material is produced by the impact of a striker through a ribbon. This category includes fully-formed character *printers* (*daisy wheel*) as well as *dot matrix* printers.

**inbetween(s)** - The *frame(s)* that lies in sequence between two *keyframes*.

**inbetweening** - The *animation* technique of adding *frames* between extreme action frames, *keyframes*, or positions in the action. A type of filling-in between specific points in the progress of the action, thereby building the work from three points; the beginning, the middle, and the end. This approach is very helpful for use in maintaining control of the action. *Computer animation programs* have the capability of *inbetweening* by extrapolating a smooth and lifelike animated movement from a drawn image at the beginning of a sequence to the final position drawn at the end of that sequence (*keyframes*), and generating the in-between frames.

**in-camera effects** - Any method of combining all elements or images to be photographed onto one piece of film or videotape, using the camera rather than post-production techniques, like re-photography or optical and electronic effects.

**incident light** - The light falling on an object. The color of an object is perceived as a function of the wavelengths of *incident light* reflected by it.

**inferiors** - *Type* characters within the same *font* but smaller in size than the text type and positioned below the baseline, as used in scientific notation of formula. Also known as "subscript".

**information center** - A large *computer* that serves *data processing* needs, as well as the main *memory* and controller of decentralized *terminals* and smaller computers in a *network*.

**Information International Inc** - One of the early pioneering *digital computer animation* production companies, founded by John Whitney Sr. Also known as *III*, or *Triple I*.

**initial letter** - An oversized type character, used at the beginning of a paragraph for effect.

**ink jet** - A printing and plotting technology in which minute, high speed, stream(s) of ink are directed onto the paper by the *print head* to form the lines and characters. As there is no direct contact with the paper by the print head, non impact *ink jet* printers are much quieter in operation than impact type *daisywheel* and *dot matrix* printers.

**input** - The raw *data*, text or commands inserted into a *computer*.

**input devices** - The five classes of input devices are: *keyboards*, locators, picks, valuators and buttons. They are represented by *devices* such as: *graphics tablets*, *light pens*, *digitizers*, a *mouse*, a *stylus*, *track balls*, and *microphones*.

**instancing** - The re-use of a previously defined geometric model (as opposed to re-defining it every time it's use is desired). A technique for defining copies of *objects* (instances) by just giving unique transformation and attribute data, and not requiring the explicit copying of the basic object *database*.

**instruction execution time** - The length of time a *computer* takes to execute an instruction.

**instruction register** - A storage location, close to the *control unit*, which contains the instructions being executed, or about to be executed.

**instruction word** - One of the components of *machine language*, it contains both an *opcode* and an *operand*.

**integers** - Whole numbers which can be positive or negative, like 534, -22, 0, 1168. They have no decimal points, denominators, or exponents to keep track of, and therefore are the easiest type of numbers to compute with.

**integrated circuit** - A *silicon chip* containing many electronic components that work as a circuit. See also, *LSI, VLSI, ULSI*.

**integrated software** - A collection of interactive *computer programs* that allow *data* to be easily transferred from one, to be used in another.

**Intelligent Light** - The name of a *developmental computer animation* production facility in the USA, which also sells its *software* as a package for use by others, principally on *Apollo* workstations.

**intelligent terminal** - A terminal with local processing capability. It does not need to be connected, or *on-line* with a larger *computer* to perform certain functions. See also, *dumb terminal*.

**intensity** - The brightness of an image, or *luminance* compared to color or *chrominance*.

**interactive** - A *device*, or *computer*, or *program* which provides immediate, or very quick, *real-time* response to input. ie: faster than human response time.

**Interactive Computer-Aided RGB Editor (ICARE)** - An *interactive* color editor program, developed by Donna Cox at *NCSA* and written in C, which enables scientists/artists to better explore the morphologies of their computations by customizing the local *computer's* color tables. This helps to reduce possible confusion in information resulting from too-similar color choices.

**interactive processing** - In *interactive* processing, an image, or *data*, can be modified or edited and the changes seen on the *display screen* right away, as opposed to *batch processing* in which the user must wait for the results to appear. See, *batch processing*.

**interface** - A common boundary or path between *systems* or parts of systems which allows each to accept and use *protocols*, *programs*, and commands from the other. May be accomplished by *software* or *hardware*.

**interfacing** - Those elements that enable one *computer system* to accept the *protocols* of another in such a way that *data* or *programs* designated for one system are useable on the other.

**interlacing** - Scanning technique which refreshes first the even, then the odd lines, or *field*, of a *display* in the refresh cycle. This reduces *flickering*.

**interpolation** - The calculation of a smooth transition from one value to another. In graphics, 1) The finding of the coordinates of a point on a curve between two, or more, known points. 2) *Computers* usually store images as numbers that represent the intensity of the image at discrete points. It is frequently necessary to determine the intensity of the image between those discrete points. *Interpolation* is a mathematical technique that generates these in-between values by looking at the surrounding intensities.

**interpreter** - An *interactive* translator for a *programming language* that executes the *program* by converting each command, in turn, into instructions that the *computer* can perform. As opposed to a *compiler*, which is not interactive, and translates the entire program, which must subsequently be executed.

**intervalometer** - A gauge for controlling the time intervals between frame exposures in *time-lapse photography*.

**inverse dynamics** - A *computer animation* technique which attempts to solve equations based on the *animator's* determination of factors, such as material or physical attributes like gravity, acceleration and friction.

**inverse transformation** - The inversion of, or opposite action to, a transformation, eg: the inversion of a positive 15-degree rotation is a negative 15-degree rotation.

**I/O** - *Input/Output*. Information which moves between a computer and another *device* or *system*. *I/O* can refer to communications between *computers*, *terminals*, *disk storage devices*, and other *peripherals*.

**IPAI** - Information Processing Association of Israel.

**IPSJ** - Information Processing Society of Japan.

**iris** - The *iris* diaphragm of a lens which controls the amount of light which enters the camera.

**Iris** - The family of widely used graphics *workstations* manufactured by Silicon Graphics.

**IS** - Information systems.

**ISA** - Instrument Society of America.

**ISDN** - Integrated Services Digital Network. A technology being introduced by telephone companies worldwide that will allow any home or office to receive voice, *computer* and video signals simultaneously on existing telephone lines.

**ISO** - International Standards Organization.

**iterative** - Repetitive. Often used to imply that each succeeding *iteration*, or repetition, of a procedure will come closer to the desired result. A technique for solving a problem by repeatedly applying the same operations.

**jaggies** - See *aliasing*.

**joystick** - A hand-held lever, or control knob, that can be moved in an x-y direction to control the movements of one or more display elements on a *computer* screen. Typically used for *real-time* screen positioning.

**jump cut** - An abrupt cut causing the action in a scene or a sequence to appear to have jumped ahead.

**Julia Set** - A set of *fractal* boundaries, named after French mathematician Gaston Julia, who studied this field of mathematics during the 1910-1925 period. See also, *Mandelbrot Set*.

**justification** - The lateral spacing of words within a line so that the margins on both sides of the page, or columns, are even and parallel.

**justify** - To set, or adjust, lines of text with the words spaced in such a way that the lines are of equal length, creating even margin on both sides of the page or columns. Commonly misused as "left-justify" and "right-justify". See, *flush left/flush right*.

**kerning** - The reduction of white space between individual characters in a line of type, to produce a better visual fit. *Kerning* programs may be stored in *computer memory* to operate automatically when desired. A good word to use as a test of the kerning ability of a graphics system is "railways".

**keyboard** - A *computer input* device on which keys are pressed to generate codes representing characters, and/or commands, to control and *input* information into a computer. Generally laid out in the traditional typewriter "*QWERTY*" format for the alphabetic keys, with the addition of *function* keys and a *number pad*.

**keyframe** - In an *animation* sequence, the beginning, or ending frame of a movement or sequence. In *computer animation*, the main positions of a model along its movement path.

**keying** - A simple video effect that replaces part of an existing screen picture with another image entirely. In *chromakeying*, a single color signal (usually blue) is removed to accommodate new visual information. A graphics computer can send out its own internal key signal to cut the required spaces in the original image, so the new visual information can fit.

**kernel** - A small but very essential task in a larger *program*. Usually it is the task which consumes most of the execution time, even though it is described with just a small amount of *program* text.

**kernel MFLOPS** - *Computer* performance on some simple, concentrated task such as summing-up a list of numbers.

**kilobyte (KB)** - $2^{10}$, or 1,024 *bytes*. A not quite accurate adaptation from metric terminology, where "kilo" is the term for one thousand.

**Kodalith** - A *high contrast* sheet film produced by Kodak. The term is often used generically to refer to any high-contrast film element.

**Labanotation** - A form of notation for recording human movement, developed and used for choreographing dancers, and which is now also being used as a basis for representing human movements in *computer animation*.

**Lambert shading** - One of the first shading models used in computer graphics, based on the application of *Lambert's* cosine law, which deals with the intensity of reflected light, discovered in the sixteenth century by Johann Lambert, a physicist and astronomer. Also referred to as "the cosine shader". See also, *flat shading*.

**LAN** - *Local Area Network*.

**language** - A set of procedures with a consistent syntax that is used to communicate instructions to a *computer*, as in a *program*.

**laptop computer** - A small, lightweight, self contained, and usually fully configured, *portable computer*, that weighs under fifteen pounds, and is equipped with a flat *screen*. Often available with a battery power source.

**laser printer** - A high speed, high quality *printer* that forms high resolution (300-1200 dpi) dot matrices with a laser beam.

**latent image** - A film printing technique used to create multiple *first generation* images on one piece of film, usually by the use of *mattes* to block-out visual information. The motion picture equivalent of a still photography double exposure.

**LCD** - *Liquid crystal display*.

**leading** - The space between lines of *type*.

**LED** - Light emitting diode.

**library** - A stored collection of tested *software* routines that are ready for use by a wide variety of *programs*.

**light box** - A box or stand, having a translucent, "frosted glass" panel that is lit from within (or underneath) by a dedicated light source. Used to illuminate photographic images or pieces of artwork for viewing or photography. In *cel animation*, a drawing desk with a rotatable drawing disc. It is lit from underneath and is used to trace a new drawing from the previous one in the sequence.

**light pen** - A photo-sensitive, hand-held *device* that can be pointed at a graphic display (*CRT*), and will send back a pulse when it senses the electron beam drawing the image. With the provision of suitable *software*, images can be created, moved or deleted, or items chosen from an on-screen *menu*.

**light source** - A "smart" *computer graphics/animation* effect that gives the appearance of a light shining on a three-dimensional object in *screen space*, with appropriate reflections, color shadings and shadows. More than one *light source* can be applied to an image at one time.

**LIM/EMS** - Lotus/Intel/Microsoft Expanded Memory Specifications.

**limited animation** - A film or sequence in which there is comparatively little full *animation*. It is therefore faster, and much cheaper to make.

**line** - The extension, in one direction, of a *point*. The shortest distance between two points.

**line filter** - An electronic device for removing unwanted *noise*, static and other various fluctuations from electrical power lines or communications lines.

**Linda** - A *parallel processing language* developed by David Gelerntere at Yale's Department of Computer Science, based on the C programming language with four extensions, and the use of *tuple space*. It is used for controlling parallel processing systems, or it can perform parallel processing using numbers of *computers* connected together.

**line spacing** - The number of lines-per-inch in a written document.

**linear address space** - In *computers*, linear memory space can be addressed sequentially.

**linear equation solver** - A *program* which solves several equations involving several unknowns. Large-scale *scientific computing* frequently involves the solution of thousands of equations in thousands of unknowns.

**linear movements** - Movements at a constant speed, in which the same distance, or the same angle, is moved every frame.

**linear system solver** - See, *linear equation solver*.

**line discipline** - The control of *data* movement across the communication line.

**line index table (LIT)** - A *hardware* pointer that points to the beginning and ending address locations of each scanline in the *frame store*.

**line printer** - A *printer* that prints an entire line of characters at one time.

**line test** - Also called *pencil test*. A run-through, or filming/recording, of an *animation* production or sequence, in "line" or *wireframe* mode, to check action, timing and positioning. As the frames do not have to be fully *rendered*, a *line test* can be done relatively quickly and inexpensively. In traditional animation, a *line test* is performed when all the pencil drawings of the various frames are completed. See also, *motion test*.

**line-up** - The setting-up of a shot or sequence in the camera.

**links** - Software tools that allow heterogeneous *database* management programs to share files.

**Links 1** - A unique *computer animation* system developed by Koichi Omura and the Toyo Links Corporation of Japan, which uses many specially designed processing units, *parallel processing* and *ray tracing* techniques to model images with points of light.

**lip sync** - The synchronization of lip movements of an animated character so they represent the natural human movements required by the dialogue being spoken.

**liquid crystal display (LCD).** A flat *display*, composed of a special liquid, sandwiched between two pieces of glass and polarisers, which forms characters and symbols by being turned from opaque to transparent as discrete electrical current is applied.

**Lisp** - List Processor. A high-level *computer programming language* in which the fundamental *data* type is a list. *Lisp* is currently the dominant language for *AI* and *Symbolic* computing applications.

**Lisp machine** - A single-user *computer* that uses a variety of special *hardware* and microcode features to optimize the execution of *programs* written in *Lisp*.

**live action** - Photographing real motion, objects or people as opposed to animated characters.

**liveware** - *Computer* personnel. Those who work with *software* and *hardware*, etc.

**loader** - A *program* which brings another program into a *computer* so that it can be run.

**local area network (LAN)** - A communications system in which a group of *microcomputers* and *peripheral devices* are linked together through *hardware* and *software* to allow *data* and resource sharing among the members (also called *nodes*) of the *LAN*.

**local intelligence** - Processing power and memory capacity built into a *terminal* so that it does not need to be connected to a *host computer* to perform certain tasks.

**local operator** - See *neighbourhood operator*.

**logic hyphenation** - A set of logical rules used by a *computer*, usually supplied by *word processing* software, to determine where to hyphenate words at line endings.

**logic-seeking** - The ability of a *printer's printhead* to discern the quickest route to its next printing position, thereby saving printing time.

**logo** - A company's corporate symbol, or its name always appearing in the same distinctive typeface.

**Logo** - A *computer programming* language that is easily learned by beginners.

**logo flops** - See *flops*.

**lookup table (LUT)** - A table of color values. *Computer graphics systems* with a small dynamic range *display* often incorporate an *LUT*. The logical colors contained in the system's *frame buffer* address the physical colors contained in the LUT, which are displayed on the *screen*. This allows a large *palette* of colors to be used although only a few can be displayed at any one time (eg: 256 from 16.7 million is typical). LUTs also allow useful *image processing* techniques and visual effects. LUT table entries can be modified (LUT animation) allowing examination of subtle effects in *scientific visualization* and *image processing*. These effects can be very pleasing and have been integrated into commercial animations. See also, *color map*.

**loop** - A series of animated *frames* showing a specific action, which are *looped* together, either physically (spliced), or within the *computer system*, so the action can be continuously repeated as required, eg: a *walk cycle* in *character animation*. Also, a *loop* of some continuous recorded sound effect which can be faded in or out as required during the editing or recording process.

**loosely-coupled** - Referring to *devices* which take a relatively long time to communicate with one another. Systems of *loosely-coupled processors* are limited to *coarse-grained* parallelism.

**lower case (type)** - Uncapitalized letters.

**low pass filter** - A *hardware* or *software* process that enhances low spatial frequencies and/or attenuates high spatial frequencies. Used to reduce *noise* in an image. Also a technique for softening an image, see also, *diffusion filter*.

**low power television** - An inexpensive television delivery system. Low or high frequency signals are sent to a small area determined by the size of the antenna and the power of its signals.

**LPM** - Lines Per Minute. A measure of a typesetting computer's, or a line-printer's, speed, based on standard newspaper lines.

**LSI** - Large Scale Integration. Refers to the quantity of electronic components and *integrated circuits* contained by a *silicon chip*. See also, *VLSI, ULSI.*

**Lumen** - A measure of light intensity. The amount of luminous flux on a 1-square-foot area of a 1-foot radius sphere cast by a 1-cd light source at the center.

**luminance** - The amount of radiant energy per unit area as measured objectively. Indicates the light intensity without the color. The subjective synonym is *brightness*.

**lustre** - The property of a surface that determines how reflective, or shiny, it is.

**Mac, MacII** - Apple Computer's *Macintosh* line of *personal computers*.

**machine language** - Coded language used directly by a *computer*, in which all commands are expressed as series of the *binary* digits "1" and "0". Thus, a *machine language program* is a set of instructions which a computer can recognize readily and directly, without intermediate interpretation or translation. Usually machine specific. See also, *binary code, binary numbers*.

**machine readable** - Encoded in *digital* format.

**Macintosh** - A relatively powerful, graphics oriented, *personal computer* manufactured by Apple Computer Corporation. Its *icon* based, on-screen *menu* system operating environment has become a standard of reference for user-interface systems of this type.

**macro** - An abbreviation for a set of *computer* instructions, usually encoded in *software*. Although the instruction list can be quite long, it is invoked by the use of a short keyword or statement.

**MAGI** - Mathematical Applications Group Inc, developers of the proprietary *Synthavision computer animation* system.

**magnetic core** - An obsolete form of main *memory* in a *computer* in which the "1" and "0" *bits* are designated by changing the magnetic polarity of tiny ferrite rings. See also, *core (storage)*.

**magnetic drum** - Recording medium using a magnetically coated metal cylinder which spins within a jacket containing a number of read/write heads. It provides faster access time, but less storage capacity, than moving-head *discs*.

**magnetic resonance imaging (MR or MRI)** - Magnetic resonance is a medical technique that uses magnetic fields rather than x-rays for non-invasive investigation. *Magnetic resonance data* can then be converted to graphics or *animation* displays using image converters such as the *Pixar*.

**magnetic tape** - Acetate or mylar ribbons coated with iron oxide which, when polarized with a magnet to represent "plus" or "minus", can be used to store *data* in *binary* format ("1", "0"). While magnetic tape can contain a high *density* of information, it is a serial storage method and lacks the *random access* capability of *disc* type storage.

**magnetic track (mag track)** - A sound track applied to a movie film by means of *analog*, or *digital* encoding of a magnetic track applied along one edge of the film stock. Also refers to a separate magnetic film tape that contains the sound track, separate from the film stock.

**magnify** - To enlarge part of an image.

**mainframe** - A large, general purpose, central *computer* which acts as host to many user *terminals* and other smaller computers, *printers*, *disc drives*, *tape drives*, etc.

**main memory** - The *computer's* high-speed internal memory which is addressed directly by the *CPU*, also known as *RAM* or *core* memory. It is usually volatile memory, which means the contents will be lost if the machine's power is interrupted, or shut-off.

**make-up** - Assembly of typeset matter and artwork into finished page(s).

**Mandelbrot, Benoit** - A mathematician who coined the term *"fractal"* in 1975, and discovered the *Mandelbrot Set* in 1980.

**Mandelbrot Set** - The set of all the *Julia Sets*. A domain in the set of *complex numbers* which produce chaotic *fractals*, or self similar spirals and whorls, when simple *iterative* procedures are applied to them.

**mapping** - A computer graphics technique for taking a two-dimensional image and applying (*mapping*) it as a surface onto a three-dimensional object. There are five main kinds of maps: 1) *texture map*, which deals with colors and textures; *bump map*, which deals with physical surfaces (normal *perturbation*); *reflection map* (or environment map), which deals with reflections; *refraction map*, which deals with refractions and transparencies; *chrome map*, for airbrush chrome simulation. Maps can be mixed on most *systems*.

**markup** - The marking of manuscript copy to indicate how it should be typeset. The insertion of *machine codes* into *computer* or *word processor* generated manuscript copy to instruct the typesetter, or *printer*, how it should be formatted.

**mass storage** - A non-volatile *memory* storage device, such as a magnetic *tape* or *disc*.

**math library** - A collection of *software* routines which perform the most important, and common, large mathematical operations required by applications *programs*, thereby eliminating having to re-specify the routine every time it has to be used.

**matrix** - In computer graphics, a square *array* of values (3 x 3 for 2-D and 4 x 4 for 3-D) that can define a unique geometric transformation, including *translation*, *scale* and *rotation*.

**matrix algebra** - An algebra of operations on *matrices* and *vectors* that is used in *computer graphics* for handling *transformations*.

**matrix multiply** - Two *matrices*, representing *transformations*, can be multiplied together to produce a third matrix which defines the *concatenation* of the two transformations. In this way, complex orientations can be efficiently handled in *computer graphics* and *animation*. Larger scale matrices are used in mathematical and scientific *simulation*. They can be very time-consuming, particularly in their use of *floating-point arithmetic*, and are often used to exercise and test arithmetic *hardware*.

**matrix vector multiply** - When a *vector* is multiplied by a *matrix*, it undergoes the unique geometric *transformation* defined by that matrix.

**matrix printer** - Usually referred to as a *dot matrix printer*, which produces images formed by dots which conform to a set *matrix* of shapes, forming the images to be printed.

**matrix shape** - The number of rows and columns in a *matrix* when expressed as a relation, eg: 4 x 5.

**matte** - A film term meaning a "mask". A black, opaque silhouette image used to prevent exposure in a specific area of photographic film. This allows images to be photographed or recorded separately and then combined into one image without double-exposure.

**matte line** - The outline of an image which results from the incorrect lining-up of a *matte* and its corresponding image.

**matte painting** - Photo-realistic art composited with live action to simulate a real setting.

**matte shot** - A shot comprised of live or other images combined with mattes.

**matting** - The process of obscuring, with a *matte*, parts of the background of an image when merging a foreground image over it.

**MCA** - *IBM's Micro Channel Architecture.*

**MDA** - Monochrome Graphics Adapter.

**measure** - The length or width of the line on which type is set. *Full measure* refers to copy set to the full width of the line. *Narrow measure* refers to indented copy.

**mechanical** - Copy and art mounted or affixed (pasted-up) in its final form, ready for the camera.

**megabyte (Mbytes)** - $2^{20}$, or 1,048,576 *bytes*.

**megaflops** - See, *MFLOPS*.

**memory** - The area in a *computer* into which *data* can be entered and stored for subsequent retrieval. See also, *RAM* and *ROM*, *main*, *peripheral*, *sequential*, and *virtual memory*, and *frame buffer*.

**memory bandwidth** - The total rate at which *data* can move between *memories* and *processors*, usually measured in millions of *bytes* per second (MB/s).

**memory interface** - The connecting logic between a *processor* and its *memory*. The more advanced *microprocessors* integrate the memory interface along with the processor.

**menu** - A list displayed on the *CRT* of a *computer*, or on the *display* of a peripheral, which offers various specific options and commands which can be selected for the operation of the *computer*, the *program* it is running, or the *peripheral*.

**menu bar** - A strip at the top of the *computer screen* containing *menu* titles and instructions for the selected function.

**menu driven** - A *computer*, *device*, or *program* which is controlled by a predetermined set of instructions and options (*menu*), rather than by the user having to develop these instructions him/herself by *programming*. This simplifies computer operation for non-experts. See also, *Smalltalk*, *WIMP*.

**metamorphosis** - The change, over a varying period of time, from an object of one shape to an object of another shape.

**MFLOPS** - Millions of Floating-Point Operations Per Second. Usually pronounced as "*megaflops*", it is the most widely-used measure of imaging and scientific *computer* speed. *Floating-point* calculations make all calculations more accurate, including x and y clipping and *z-axis* determination, but require computer power. Megaflops are a measure of floating-point performance, not *CPU* speed, and are only useful for comparing general-purpose computers. On a graphics *workstation*, *MFLOPS* determine the ability to transform the vertices of the image, and the speed of moving a complex object around the screen. See also, *GFLOPS*.

**MGA** - Monochrome Graphics Adapter.

**Micro Channel Architecture (MCA)** - *IBM's* new 32-*bit bus* architecture design as used on its PS/2 line of *personal computers*.

**microcode** - Low-level *programming*, or microprogramming, which defines the basic operations of a *computer*. It is usually set by the manufacturer and inaccessible to the user.

**microcomputer** - A small *computer* containing a *microprocessor*, *memory*, *input* and *output* and a *display* all in one case, or in three closely-connected pieces of equipment, referred to as a *desk-top*, *portable*, or *laptop* unit. It may have other *peripherals* (eg: *printer*, *digitizer*) attached to it, it may be *interfaced* with a *host* computer, or it may be connected to other *microcomputers* via a *network*.

**microprocessor** - A single *chip* or *integrated circuit* containing the entire *central processing unit (CPU)* of a computer.

**MIDI** - *Musical Instrument Digital Interface*.

**MIMD** - Multiple Instruction, Multiple Data.

**Mindset** - A small title generator with an optional *paint* system, no longer being marketed.

**miniature** - A scale model.

**minicomputer** - Smaller than a *mainframe*, less expensive, and generally less powerful, *minicomputers* have largely been supplanted by more powerful *mini-supercomputers* and super-microcomputers.

**mini-supercomputer** - A *computer* whose speed and architecture resemble the *supercomputers* of the previous generation, but is usually contained in a much smaller "package". *Mini-supercomputers* are often designed to be more adept at specific types of processing tasks (eg: a graphics computer), and can generally perform those specific tasks as fast as, or faster than, a *supercomputer*.

**MIPS** - Million Instructions Per Second. A measure of a *computer's CPU* processing power or speed. See also, *MFLOPS*.

**Mirage** - A three-dimensional digital image manipulator, with a "floating" viewpoint, made by *Quantel*.

**MIS** - Management Information System. A *computer system* designed to provide information, usually from a central *database*, on the progress or status of various operations.

**misconvergence** - The improper alignment of the three *(RGB)* electron beams of a color *monitor*, or a *CRT*.

**mixing** - In film/video - *mixing* or *dissolving* one scene into the next. In Audio - *mixing* or *dubbing* several sound/voice tracks into one track.

**mnemonic** - Assisting, or designed to aid, the memory. In *computer* use, abbreviations of complex terms used to reduce the work of encoding *computer* instructions. Most symbolic assembly languages use mnemonic operation codes which are typically abbreviations of words, such as MPY for multiply, and SUB for subtract.

**model** - A three-dimensional representation built to scale. Can refer to either a "solid", "real" *model*, or a *computer* generated model defined by the *animator*, which exists only in the computer's *memory*.

**modeling** - An abstract, mathematical description of a graphic object that a *computer* can translate into a two-dimensional or three-dimensional display. The act of creating an object with the aid of a *computer system* by defining its shape, dimensions, color and surface texture.

**modem** - A contraction of "modulator-demodulator". A device that provides an *interface* between a *computer* (and/or a *data* processing machine, *system,* or remote *terminal*) with a communications line. It translates computer data into pulses/signals, allowing the transfer of data between computers etc, over regular telephone lines or optical cables.

**modular** - Divided into functional units so that specific combinations can be made to best suit a given job.

**modulation** - The process of impressing information on any electromagnetic signal at a particular frequency, to allow transmission over a distance. Used for transmission of *data*, voice or image information.

**moire pattern** - an unintentional, and undesirable, pattern on a video *screen (CRT)* arising from a variety of causes. Mostly as a consequence of inadequate sampling and therefore closely related to *aliasing. Anti aliasing* techniques can often be successfully applied.

**Molcad** - An *interactive* molecule display program for three-dimensional manipulations of structures and molecular properties. Written in C for use on *workstations,* there also is a simplified version available for the Amiga *personal computer.* Developed at the Institut fur Physikalische Chemie in Darmstadt, West Germany.

**monitor** - A *CRT* unit and its housing.

**monochrome** - A single color.

**monochrome display** - A *monitor* that displays information and images in a single color, such as green on a black background. It generally has a higher *resolution* than a color monitor and is therefore more suitable for *data processing* and *word processing* use, which require long periods of user viewing.

**mono conversion** - Converting a color image *input* into a black-and-white image.

**MOP** - Motion picture language. A three-dimensional *computer animation* system developed by Edwin Catmull in 1972, at the University of Utah.

**motherboard** - The main system board in a *computer*, particularly a *personal computer*, which carries the *CPU* and main *bus*, and to which the various auxiliary system cards and boards, disk drives and peripherals are attached.

**motion blur** - The technique of imparting a *software* generated localized elongation, or blurring effect, to a *computer* generated *character*, or *object*, so as to give it the appearance of rapid acceleration and motion as it moves within a scene. A solution for *temporal aliasing*.

**motion control system** - A horizontal, computerized camera system in which artwork or *miniature models* can be articulated and made to move in a natural manner through the five axes of motion. The *camera* moves along a horizontal track in the *zoom* axis. The *computer* permits precise control and repeatability of moves on the various axes. It also controls other motion control systems, such as an articulated mechanical arm, and regulates camera functions such as focus and shutter action.

**motion graphics** - See *animation*.

**motion path** - The path a *model*, or object, will follow over the course of an animation.

**motion test** - This is the *computer animation* equivalent of the traditional *animation pencil test*. It is a preliminary run-through of an animated sequence to check the timing and confirm whether or not the motion and movement of the objects will work as planned. A *motion test*, in conjunction with a *color test (wedge)* provides the information necessary to proceed with the production.

**mouse** - A small, hand held device that is moved over a surface and which, by its position and motion, provides coordinate input to the *computer*, which is used to calculate the position of a *cursor* on the *display device*. Usually equipped with up to three buttons for selecting information or instigating action on the computer screen.

**Movie.Byu** - A *program* used to describe models of three-dimensional objects. Although it has been used as the base of some commercial *computer animation programs*, it is now primarily used in university and other non-commercial settings.

**Movieola** - A film editing machine made by the Movieola Company. The term is also often used in reference to any film editing machine.

**MR, MRI** - *Magnetic Resonance Imaging.*

**MS-DOS** - Microsoft Disk Operating System. A widely used *personal computer operating system* developed by Microsoft Corporation.

**MSGEN** - A *keyframe* based *computer animation* system developed by N Burtnyk and M Wein in 1971, at the National Research Council of Canada.

**multibus** - A standardized *bus* used in some *computers*.

**Multiple Instruction, Multiple Data (MIMD)** - A *parallel processing* scheme, more difficult to *program* than *SIMD*, but more flexible in how many *algorithms* can be employed.

**multiple passes** - The process of exposing multiple images on one frame of film or videotape by exposing, rewinding and exposing the frame again.

**multiplex** - To interleave, and thereby simultaneously transmit, two or more messages or *data* streams, on one communications channel.

**multiprogramming** - Running two or more *programs* in a *computer* so they appear to the user to be executing at the same time.

**multiprocessing** - The use of more than one *processor* in a *computer*, which allows a single job or task to run faster, or multiple jobs to be run simultaneously.

**multitasking** - Handling more than one job or task at a time, either by taking turns on a single *processor*, or by using different processors for each job.

**music track** - The sound track of a musical recording.

**Musical Instrument Digital Interface (MIDI)** - A standard format for *digital* information that allows electronic musical instruments to communicate with each other, and with *computers*.

**MUTAN** - Multiple Track Animator. An interactive system for independently animating three-dimensional graphic objects, developed by D Fortin in 1983.

**MWords** - Millions of **words** of memory. Large scale imaging and scientific computing demands *MFLOPS* of speed and *MWords* of storage.

**native language** - In *computer* use, refers to the set of commands which are the low-level operations performed by the *device*. Other *languages* can be used, but first they must be translated to that set of operations.

**NBS** - National Bureau of Standards, USA.

**NCC** - National Computer Conference, USA.

**NCGA** - National Computer Graphics Association, USA.

**NCSA** - National Center for Supercomputing Applications, USA.

**negative** - A photographic reproduction with normal colors or tones reversed, usually reproduced as transparent and opaque image areas. Used in *computer animation* as a shadow effect.

**neighbourhood operator** - A procedure applied to a *pixel* that incorporates information about the pixels that surround and touch it. See also, *global operator, point operator*.

**neon** - The diffused-glow lighting effect produced by tubular *neon* gas filled electrical discharge lamps. Glows and highlights are used to achieve a similar "tubular electronic lighting" effect in *computer animation*. Used for its "high-tech" look.

**network** - A system consisting of a *computer* and its connected *terminals* and *devices*. Several computers can also be *networked* together, enabling them to share *programs* and *data*.

**neural networks** - *Computer systems* that are designed to imitate the way a human nervous system (brain) computes.

**NeXT** - An innovative, *Unix* based, *personal computer* system introduced in 1988 by NeXT Inc.

**NG** - Unacceptable, as in "no good".

**NGI** - Netherlands Society for Informatics.

**NMR** - *Nuclear Magnetic Resonance*.

**nodal point** - Central point on the axis of movement.

**node** - Intersecting corner of a *polygon*.

**nodes** - Stations on a *local area network (LAN)*.

**noise** - Any unwanted random variation in a signal which can interfere with its information content. In a picture, *noise* refers to abnormal or spurious *pixel* values, whatever their source. High frequency noise is sometimes added to an image to reduce *aliasing*. See, *dithering*.

**non interlaced** - Scanning method that refreshes all lines on a *CRT display* from top-to-bottom in sequential order, usually at a rate of 60 times per second. This reduces *flicker*.

**non-uniform rational B-spline (NURBS)** - An optionally rational curve with user-specified order, non-uniform knot *vector* and control points. A *NURBS* is a special kind of *spline* which features the ability to model quadratic curves such as circles.

**north/south** - The vertical axis of movement.

**normal** - Relating to the orientation of a surface, a *normal* specifies the direction it is facing, or its orientation to the viewer. A *vector* at right angles to the surface, ie: normal vector, or vector normal.

**NTSC** - National Television Standards Committee. A "standard" color encoding scheme used for analog television broadcast and video displays in North, Central and South America, and Japan.

**NuBus** - Apple Computer's 32 *bit bus* architecture.

**Nuclear Magnetic Resonance** - A non-invasive, medical imaging technique which produces images based on extremely fine differences emitted by the atomic structure of the body when it is placed in a magnetic field. *NMR* is safer than *CAT* scanning because it does not rely on potentially harmful x-rays, yet it produces equal, or better images.

**number cruncher** - A slang term for a powerful *computer*.

**number pad** - A dedicated area on a *computer keyboard* that contains keys for the numbers 0-9, positioned in the standard calculator "3-row plus 0" layout with various operator keys, allowing one-handed *input* of numerical data at a faster rate than allowed by the regular *QWERTY* alpha-numeric keyboard. Also available as a separate, plug-in *number pad* unit for computers without number pads.

**NURBS** - *Non-uniform rational B-spline.*

**NVRAM** - Non-volatile *random access memory*. *NVRAM* will not be lost if the power is switched-off or interrupted. See also, *main memory*.

**NYIT** - New York Institute of Technology.

**nybble** - A unit of *storage* consisting of half a *byte*, usually four *bits*.

**object** - The representation of a thing or a concept to a *computer*. ie: a line, circle or *polygon* which can be isolated and moved. Also used to refer to a three-dimensional entity.

**object-oriented programs** - *Programs* that are divided into *objects* - small modules that contain both programming instructions and *data*. Since the modules or objects are completely separate from one another, object oriented programs are easy to modify.

**OCR** - Optical Character Recognition. An electronic means, usually in the form of a *device,* for scanning copy, and converting it to an electronic equivalent that is recognizable, and useable, by a *computer.*

**occultation** - The determination of the surfaces and edges of a three-dimensional object that would be visible from a viewer's point of view and not occluded by other nearer objects, and only showing those. See also, *hidden line removal* and *hidden surface removal.*

**OEM** - Original Equipment Manufacturer. Companies that purchase components to add to products they "manufacture" before distributing them. See also, *VAR.*

**off-line** - Equipment that is not in direct communication with the central *processor (CPU)* of a *computer system*, as opposed to *devices* directly connected to it, and which therefore are *on-line.*

**on-line** - Equipment that is in direct communication, and connected to, the central *processor (CPU)* of a *computer system*, as opposed to *off-line.*

**OODB** - Object-oriented database.

**OODBMS** - Object-Oriented Database Management System.

**opacity** - The capacity of a material to obstruct the viewing of objects which lie behind it. The opposite of *transparency.*

**opaque overlay** - An overlay or plane that prevents any background information from being seen.

**opcode** - Specifies the functionality in an *instruction word*, such as the functions +, or -, and is represented in *binary* code.

**open** - In *computer* terminology, to retrieve a file from *storage*, make a *window* available for viewing, or make a *tool* available for use.

**Open Look** - A new *graphical user interface (GUI)* announced by AT&T in April 1988, destined to be the GUI for *Unix* System V, version 4.0. Designed to be independent of the *hardware* and *software* on which it runs, *Open Look* can also be used with *operating systems* other than Unix.

**open system** - A specification available to the industry in general, so as to allow products made by several manufacturers to be compatible and work together. Usually accomplished by conforming to internationally recognized standards established by industry groups.

**operand** - The *data*, or quantities acted upon by an operation. When one computes A=B+C, quantities B and C are *operands*.

**operating system (OS)** - The *software*, or master control *program*, which manages all other tasks, keeping all of the components of a *computer system* working harmoniously together, such as *MS-DOS* or *Unix*.

**optical disc** - See *CD-ROM*.

**optical fibre** - A very thin, flexible fibre of pure glass that transmits information as pulses of light generated by a *laser* or a *light emitting diode (LED)*. It can carry much more information than comparably sized copper wire.

**optical print** - A film print made on an *optical printer* as opposed to a contact printer.

**optical printer** - A *device* for recording images directly to photographic (movie) film, consisting basically of a projector, or a *high-resolution display (CRT)*, and a camera, with a single lens between them. Used for producing special effects such as fades, dissolves, wipes, split screens, composite matte shots, etc.

**opticals** - A term used to refer to the various effects produced with the aid of an *optical printer*.

**optical scanner** - A *device* which analyzes the light reflected from, or transmitted through, copy, artwork or film images, and then produces a *digital* signal proportional to the intensity of the light or color.

**optical track** - A film sound track consisting of optical markings positioned along one edge of the film stock. These are "read" by the *projector's* optical scanner and translated into sounds (music, speech, etc).

**origin** - The point of intersection of the axis in *Cartesian* coordinate systems. A reference point whose coordinates are all zero.

**original** - The master negative or copy of a film from which the various *generation* copies are made.

**orthogonal** - A view of an object showing no perspective.

**OSF** - The Open Software Foundation. A consortium of *computer* and *software* manufacturers and suppliers which is charged with developing an industry-standard, *Unix*-based, operating system.

**OSF/MOTIF** - A *graphical user interface (GUI)*, the first product of the *OSF*, comprised of a *window* manager and *tool kit*. It is being made available to system/software manufacturers to enable easy and standard user *interfaces* with their products.

**OS/2** - *IBM's* proprietary "second generation" *operating system* for its *personal computers*. Developed for IBM by Microsoft as a replacement for *IBM-DOS*, IBM's version of *MS-DOS*.

**outline characters** - Open *type* characters which are defined only by lines around their edges.

**output** - The material produced by a *device*, such as a *computer*, *printer*, video recorder, or *plotter*.

**overcrank** - The process of filming or video recording at speeds faster than standard (ie: 24 and 30 frames-per-second respectively), to produce a slow-motion effect when played-back at regular speeds.

**overlay** - To temporarily transfer all, or a portion, of one *program* from auxiliary *storage* into the central storage, so it can be used in conjunction with the main program already running. This allows programs that are larger than the central *memory* to be executed, although the execution is necessarily slow. In art/animation, to put one piece of artwork, or image, over another, so they can be moved independently while being photographed together. See also, *virtual memory*.

**Oxberry** - A company that produces film and video *animation stands*. The name is now often used generically to refer to any animation stand.

**Pacific Data Images (PDI)** - A well known North American *developmental computer animation* production facility which uses its own proprietary software.

**packet switching** - A method of *data* communications in which the message is split up into smaller units, transmitted and reassembled at the other end. Each packet may be sent by a different route.

**page** - That area of a *computer memory* large enough to store a complete image.

**pagination** - The integration of text, illustrations and pictures into a whole page.

**PAINT** - The "industry basic" *paint system* developed by Alvy Ray Smith in 1976, at *NYIT*. It allows an artist to paint by using a *stylus* and *digitizing tablet* while watching the results on a color *monitor*.

**Paintbox** - Trademarked name for the widely used *paint system* manufactured by *Quantel*. Its features include extensive paint simulation, video-image retouching and some three-dimensional image manipulation. "*Paintbox*" is now often used to refer to any paint system.

**paint system** - A *computer* graphics system that allows an artist to draw directly into the computer's *frame buffer*, and color those drawings, which are displayed on the *CRT,* and can be stored, printed, or transferred to video or other recording *device*. Generally consists of a *digitizing tablet* and *stylus*, *frame buffer*, and control computer, and may simulate various art media such as watercolor, oil, gouache, etc. All digital *paint systems* today are direct descendants of the *Superpaint* system developed by Richard Shoup in 1973, which was followed by the "industry basic" *PAINT* system developed by Alvy Ray Smith during the mid-'70s at *NYIT*.

**PAL** - Phase Alternating Line. A video system in which the subcarrier phase is inverted from one *raster* line to the next. *PAL* is the television broadcast standard used in most of Western Europe. It has a higher number of *scan lines* (625 per frame at 50Hz) than *NTSC (512)*, and therefore delivers a higher *resolution* picture.

**palette** - Generally, the assortment of colors being used, or stored, when creating a computer generated image. The term may also be used to refer to an on-screen color *menu* or, occasionally, to the *digitizing tablet*. See also, *lookup table (LUT)*.

**pan (panorama, panning)** - The movement of the camera across a field of view, horizontally, vertically or diagonally.

**parallel interface** - A method of sending *data* from a *computer* to another *device*, whereby one entire *byte*, or *word*, of information is usually sent at one time, each bit in parallel along its own wire or data path.

**parallel port** - A communications *device* that can send or receive one entire *byte*, or *word*, of information at a time.

**parallel processing** - *Multiprocessing* in which the processors execute tasks almost simultaneously. *Parallel processing* can significantly reduce the computing time required for a specific job.

**parallel processors** - A group of *computer processors* which operate all at the same time, as opposed to sequential, or *pipelined* processors.

**parallel transfer disc (PTD)** - A type of *disc* storage system specialized for high-performance, in which multiple *data* streams are transferred in parallel. Enables quick access to large *databases* for generally *real-time* analysis, or real-time display of digital video sequences as in *Harry*.

**parameters** - A fixed limit, guideline or specification, such as object size, range of movement, type size, etc. In mathematics, a constant whose value determines the operation of a system.

**parametric surface patch** - A way of describing three-dimensional objects, using a limited number of control points to define the shape and curve of the object's surface.

**particle system** - A *simulation, animation* and *rendering* system in which images are composed of particles of varying width, length, color and transparency, which are rendered with *anti-aliasing, motion blur* and *hidden surface removal*. Acceleration, velocity and position of the particles are animated with dynamic simulation to create physically realistic looking motion. Various operations, or properties, can be applied to selected sets of particles to govern their movements, such as gravity and weight. Invented by Bill Reeves at Lucasfilm.

**partitioning** - Dividing a problem into smaller pieces, so that many processors can work on it simultaneously. Also, dividing a *storage device*, such as a *hard disc*, into *partitions* so they may be allocated to different tasks or users.

**Pascal** - A high-level *computer programming language*, named for the French mathematician Blaise Pascal.

**PC** - *Personal computer*.

**PDDI** - Product Data Definition Interchange.

**PDES** - Product Data Exchange Specification.

**PDL** - Page Description Language.

**Peak MFLOPS** - A speed rating of a computer based on all of its functional units operating under ideal conditions, which is seldom sustained in actual practice. See also, *sustained MFLOPS*.

**pencil test** - See, *motion test*.

**penetration tube, beam penetration tube** - A *cathode ray tube (CRT)* which produces different colors by the use of different levels of phosphors, and accelerating its beam to different voltages.

**percent parallel** - That portion, or percentage, of a computing job which can be rendered faster by using *parallel processors*. The effective use of parallel processors depends on making this percentage as close to 100% as possible.

**peripheral equipment (peripheral device)** - The ancillary equipment connected to the *central processing unit (CPU)* and its associated *memory* in a *computer system*, such as *input/output devices*, secondary storage units (*disc* drives), and a *CRT*.

**peripheral memory** - *Memory* storage that is not addressed directly by the *computer*, but instead resides in a *peripheral device*.

**persistence** - The time it takes for the light given off by the phosphor in a *CRT display* to decay to ten percent (10%) of its peak value. Long *persistence phosphors* emit light for a longer period of time after electron beam stimulation ceases. This reduces *flicker* on static displays, but causes "trails" on moving objects.

**personal computer (PC)** - General purpose, relatively low-cost, desk-top (or *laptop*, or *portable*) computers that use 8-, 16- or 32-*bit microprocessors*. The latest, most powerful versions are based on the Intel 80386 microprocessor operating at 25 MHz.

**perspective** - The art of depicting on a flat, two-dimensional surface, images that appear to have depth.

**perspective rendering** - *Computer graphics* generated from a three-dimensional *database*, but displayed two-dimensionally.

**perturbation** - A method of making *simulations* more natural by introducing an initial change, a *perturbation*, into the sequence, which then generates other actions and reactions. See also, *bump mapping*.

**PET** - *Positron Emission Tomography*.

**PHIGS** - Programmer's Hierarchical Graphics Standard. The latest version of this standard for real-time, three-dimensional graphics generation is called *PHIGS+*.

**Phong shading** - A smooth shading technique, developed by Phong Bui-Tuong in 1975. *Phong interpolates* the *surface normal* at each *pixel*, and does an individual illumination calculation at each step. *Phong* is more accurate than *Gouraud*, but is computationally much more intensive, and can be hundreds of times slower to calculate. "Fast *Phong*", which is claimed to approach *Gouraud's* speed, uses a *lookup table* to avoid computing each pixel.

**phosphor** - The chemical that is coated on the inside face, or *screen*, of a *CRT*, which emits a visible light when excited by an electron beam from an electron gun.

**phototypesetting** - The production of *type* through the use of various light sources, shaped matrices, lenses and photosensitive material, resulting in the subsequent transferal of the created characters to paper.

**pica** - A printer's unit of measurement, approximately one-sixth of an inch.

**picture archival and communication system (PACS)** - Systems being developed for the archiving of images for Medical Imaging.

**picture file** - A file within a *computer system* that contains all the *data* needed to generate an image. Typically stored on a *disc*.

**PictureMaker** - A *PC* based *computer animation* system manufactured by Cubicomp Corp. One of the earliest fully featured *turn-key* computer animation systems, *PictureMaker* is constantly upgraded and enhanced, and is one of the most widely used computer animation systems, regardless of type.

**pin feed (printer)** - A method of paper transport in which attached, continuous sheets of paper, supplied with a series of punched holes down each side, are pulled through the printer by sprockets with matching pins attached to both sides of the *platen*. If the sprockets are separate from the platen, it is referred to as a *tractor drive printer*. A method of precise, continuous paper transport and alignment suitable for high speed printing, or long, unattended printer runs.

**pipeline** - An assembly line approach for performing a task. Each "station" in the *pipeline* rapidly performs one step of the task, then passes it on to the next station.

**Pixar** - A sample-based image processor, produced by Pixar (Inc). *Pixars* produce high quality pictures based on manipulation of *pixel data* rather than geometric data, utilizing a unique parallel processor and memory architecture, and a wide range of *software toolkits*.

**pixblt** - A *bitmap* block transfer with arithmetic operations (in contrast to a *bitblt* which performs only logical operations). Can be used to achieve transparency or visual mixing of two *frame store* images. Term devised by *Pixar*, although *Quantel* claim precedence of concept. See also, *bitblt* and *pixel operations*.

**pixel** - Picture element. A *pixel* is the smallest definable visual unit of a two-dimensional image which can be shown on a *computer display* and modified or stored. *Raster scan* systems divide the screen into a two-dimensional *array* of *pixels*.

**pixel operations** - *Pixel data* is stored as numbers which are converted into color, or other information. Arithmetic and logical operations can be done on this data for filtering, image modification and other purposes.

**pixel manipulation** - Similar to *pixel operation*, but can also include moving a *pixel* to another point in the image.

**pixellization** - A video effect, produced by dividing a picture, or an image, into regular, or irregular, groups of coarse *"pixels"*, or square tile shapes, which display the averaged value of the pixels they contain.

**pixilation** - Animation of actors, objects or environments by the use of single frame photography.

**plain paper** - Usually refers to cut-sheet bond paper as used in *laser printers* and photocopiers, as opposed to *fanfold* or roll-fed computer paper, or electrostatic and thermal paper as used in *fax* machines.

**plane** - A two-dimensional surface.

**plasma panel** - See *gas plasma display*.

**plotter** - A graphic, hard copy *output* device, which uses a single, or grouping of, markers, usually fine-line pens, to trace lines and images onto sheets of paper. The plotting head and paper transport are under *computer* control, the paper can be moved forward and back, and the plotting head can also move across the paper, giving it access to the entire surface of the drawing. In small size plotters, the paper is fixed and the plotting head can move in both an x or y axis. In large plotters, the paper is in large sheets, or is roll-fed, and is moved under the plotting head, which only moves back and forth on the x axis.

**plug compatible** - A way of saying that *hardware* from one manufacturer is "just like" that from another at the signal *input/output* port - they may be very different internally, but "look" the same at the plug. *Plug compatible* indicates that a *device*, usually a *peripheral*, from one manufacturer can simply be plugged into a another manufacturer's *computer* without rewiring, programming or interfacing being required.

**point** - In graphics, the most primitive element, as it is a dimensionless entity.

**point** - In printing, a division of the *pica*. There are 12 *points* to a pica, and approximately 72 *points* to the inch.

**point-of-sale terminals** - Electronic *terminals* used at retail outlets to record financial transactions as they occur.

**point-of-view (POV)** - The position in space from which the camera, or viewer, sees a three-dimensional scene. See also, *viewpoint*.

**point operator** - A function that is applied to a *pixel* independently of other pixels in the image. See also, *global operator*, *neighbourhood operator*.

**point size** - The height of *type*, from the highest *ascender* to the lowest *descender*, with additional allowances for the *font* design.

**polar coordinates** - Coordinates which indicate the position of a point in a plane with reference to its distance from a fixed point known as the "pole", and the angle that the line joining the point to the pole makes with the fixed line, known as the "initial line". Two angles are needed for 3-D.

**polarized light** - Light whose wavelength vibrations are all in one direction.

**polyhedron** - A three-dimensional continuous solid object, such as a cube.

**polygon** - A planar geometric figure bounded by straight lines. The building-blocks of solid images, these geometric shapes are described by mathematical coordinates that identify their vertices, entered through a *computer keyboard*, or *input* via points with a *digitizing tablet*. *Polygon* generated images appear as faceted objects if *flat shading* is used, they appear smooth if *Gouraud* or *Phong* shading is used.

**polygonal modeling** - Describing the surface of an object in terms of planar *polygons*. Very good for *modeling* and recreating geometric images to exact shapes where the base data can be *input* with a *digitizing tablet*. The surfaces of spheres approximated by *polygons* are represented by numerous small flat surfaces. See also, *bicubic patch*.

**polygonal shading** - A simple shading technique which colors the face of each *polygon* with a single intensity of light and color.  See, *flat shading*.

**port** - A *computer interface*, usually in the form of *hardware* (a *board*) or special circuitry, that connects the *CPU* with various *peripherals*.  See, *parallel port, serial port*.

**portability** - The characteristic of a *program* which allows it to be used on more than one *computer system*.

**portable** - As in *portable computer*.  A relatively small and lightweight, self contained, *computer system*, complete with *display* and *disc drive(s)*.  *Portable* computers now fall into two categories; *transportables*, which are larger, usually contain *expansion slots*, often use *CRT* displays and weigh eighteen to twenty pounds or more, and *laptops*, which are considerably smaller, use flat *LCD* or *gas plasma* displays, and weigh under fifteen pounds.  *Portable* computers can now offer the same power and capabilities as desk-top *minicomputers*.

**Positron Emission Tomography (PET)** - A non-invasive, medical diagnostic and imaging technology.  See *CAT, CT* and *MR, MRI*.

**posterization** - A *digital* or *analog* effect that breaks-up an image into highly colored areas by converting *intensity* range into color values.

**post-syncing** - The recording, mostly of *dialogue*, in synchronization with the actor's, or character's lip movements after the images have been filmed or recorded.

**POV** - *Point-of-view*.

**precision** - The number of decimal points in a calculation.  Because *digital computers* don't represent *floating-point numbers precisely*, *precision* errors result.  These are a major problem, particularly in computer graphics.

**pre-press** - The stages of production for printed material, such as books and magazines, that occur prior to the actual printing process.  This includes layout, resizing, typesetting, color separations and color correction.  Much of this once tedious work can now be done by *computer*.

**presentation graphics** - Graphics intended for use in audio-visual demonstrations and business presentations.

**primary colors** - A set of colors from which all other colors are derived, but which cannot be produced from each other.  The additive *primary colors* (light based) are **red, green** and **blue**, the colors used in video displays.  The subtractive *primary colors* (pigment based) are **yellow, magenta** and **cyan**, the colors used in graphic printing.

**primitive element (primitives)** - Fundamental graphic elements, such as a point or line segment, which can readily be combined with other *primitives* to form more complex images, or objects, in two or three dimensions.

**printer** - A *device* for recording *hard copy* of *data* onto paper, either through the use of *type* (typewritten) or graphic representation. The main types of *printers* used with *computers* are *daisywheel, dot matrix, ink jet,* and *laser*.

**printhead** - The device which houses the printing mechanism in a *printer* or *plotter*.

**printout** - A paper record of a *computer's* computations, or the work it has processed.

**prioritize** - To assign a numerical measure of importance to a task, so that an *operating system* can better decide which tasks to work on first.

**priority** - In *computer animation*, the concept of giving priority to one image in a *frame* over another, so that they are in effect "stacked" , such as a *character* over a *background*. This is sometimes referred to as $2^1/_2$ dimensions, as it is based on prioritizing 2-D images and is not full 3-D.

**PRISM** - *Apollo* Computer's parallel reduced set instruction multiprocessing architecture for its super graphics *workstations*.

**PRISMS** - Three-dimensional computer animation *software*, developed by Omnibus Computer Graphics, now being further developed by Side Effects. *PRISMS* is now being used by a small number of licensees in various countries.

**process color** - Four color graphic printing, which uses yellow, magenta, cyan and black.

**program** - A complete set of instructions, in a *language* compatible with the *computer* it is to be used in. The *program* directs the computer to perform each operation at the right time and in the correct sequence.

**program counter** - A component of the *CPU* which indicates where the current instruction is stored.

**programmer** - Person who writes *programs* for *computers*.

**programming environment** - The entire set of *software tools* that is available to a user in order to facilitate *program* development. Tools available in advanced *programming environments* can include *interpreters, compilers, editors, debuggers,* file systems, *window* systems, *electronic mail, local area networks*, and extended language features like *object-oriented programming*.

**programming language** - A set of *computer* commands that form a procedure, or *language*, complete with its own syntax and structure, by which *software* programmers design and implement computer software *programs*.

**projector** - A machine used to project filmed, videotaped or televised images.

**Prolog** - A logic-based *symbolic processing* language, developed in France in 1972. Currently in use in Europe and Japan, and to a lesser extent in North America, it is now experiencing renewed interest due to its suitability for *parallel processing* applications.

**proportional spacing** - Printing in which the space on the line for each character is determined by the needs of that character, eg: an "i" requires less space than an "m". *Typesetting*, most *word processors*, and some typewriters, use *proportional spacing*, which gives the printed work a more aesthetically pleasing appearance and makes it easier to read. See also, *kerning*.

**proprietary system** - An *operating system*, or *hardware* or *software*, that only operates for a single vendor's product, the specifications for which are not available to the industry in general (vs *open system*).

**protocol** - A set of agreed-upon rules and controls followed by the *software* to establish and maintain communications. *Protocol* consists of *handshaking* and line discipline.

**pseudo-colors** - Also called false colors. Colors arbitrarily assigned, via a *lookup table (LUT)*, to an image to highlight some property or represent *data* values, rather than natural likeness or attributes. Often used in satellite imagery and scientific *visualization*. *Pseudo-colors* are typically a consequence of having only 8 *bits* for *color mapped* color, and also a consequence of LUT systems where the logical colors in the *frame buffer* are not the same as the physical colors in the lookup table.

**puck** - The hand-held device used to register input points when tracing images on a *digitizing table*. See also, *digitizing tablet, cross-hair digitizer*.

**pulldown menu** - Menus that "reside" in a bar along the top of the *screen*, and appear as overlays (*windows*) to the material on the screen when they are "pulled down" by the *cursor*. Several menus can usually be in use at any one time, each overlaying the other in order of their selection. This technique is referred to as hierarchical menu handling.

**pulse** - A discrete step on a motor, one increment of movement.

**Q-bus** - The internal *system* used in some Digital Equipment Corporation (*DEC*) MicroVAX *computers* for *data* communications.

**quad** - To space-out the blank portion of a line to its full measure.

**quadrilateral mesh** - A new primitive description defined by *PHIGS+* that defines an N x M *array* of *vertices* where each of the four neighbouring vertices defines a single, perhaps nonplanar, quadrilateral.

**Quantapaint** - *Personal computer (PC)* compatible graphics/*paint* system from Quanta, which can interface with its *character generator* line.

**Quantel** - Manufacturer of a line of *computerized paint systems* (*Paintbox*), effects generators and *digital* editors and recorders (*Harry*). (Quantel - from **quan**tised **tele**vision)

**quantization** - The process of giving each *sample* in the *digitizing* process a numerical value. The number of *bits* used to store the number will define how many *quantizing* levels are available. If too few bits are used, quantizing errors will be introduced. This is a form of *aliasing* which can be treated by *dithering*.

**QWERTY** - The standard layout of typewriter and *computer keyboard* alphabetic and numeric keys, when based on Romance language alphabets. The term comes from the top row of letters for the left hand "Q-W-E-R-T-Y". It is not the most efficient keyboard layout, having originally been designed when typewriters were first introduced as a means of preventing fast typists from jamming the keys, because they were too quick for the mechanical key transports then available. Although the *Dvorak* keyboard is much more efficient, the vast number of *Qwerty* keyboards extant, and people's lengthy experience with them, have inhibited its general use.

**qwertyuiop** - What you get when you run your finger along the second row of keys on a *computer* keyboard.

**query** - A specific request for *data* or instructions in a computerized *DBMS*.

**query by example (QBE)** - A method of making *database queries* in a graphic manner, rather than in an English-like, or programmatic manner.

**radiosity** - A technique for the photorealistic rendering of environments. *Radiosity* is based on thermal engineering techniques for determining the exchange of radiant energy between surfaces. It computes the global illumination within a scene consisting of diffusely reflecting surfaces, taking into account the geometry and material properties of all surfaces in the scene when computing the illumination at any given point.

**ragged** - Not *justified*. The setting of type with an irregular appearance at either one or both margins, usually *ragged* right margin.

**raised initial** - An initial character, usually a capital letter, which projects upward from the first line of type.

**RAM** - *Random Access Memory*.

**random access memory (RAM)** - Semiconductor *memory* in which each *byte* of storage has a unique *address* in the *system's* address map, and so can be accessed directly and not, for example, serially.

**random access storage** - *Data storage* in which *records* or individual *bytes* are accessible independent of their location in relation to the previous or following record or byte accessed.

**range** - A set of intermediate colors whose values are between two end colors.

**rapid prototyping** - *Programming* techniques that use high-level *tools* to explore the feasibility and functionality of *software* designs by developing simplified, inelegant, or inefficient, versions of the proposed program.

**raster** - Pattern of horizontal lines scanned by the electron beams in a *CRT* as it draws the image on a *screen*.

**raster data** - The representation of an image by storing its intensities or colors as a regular two-dimensional grid of *pixels*. *Raster data* images are distinct from *wireframe* or calligraphic images, where drawings are stored by saving only the endpoints of the lines. Raster data images are stored in a *frame buffer*, or *frame store*.

**raster display** - A *display device* that stores and displays *data* as a sequential series of horizontal rows of picture elements (*pixels*), such as a *cathode ray tube (CRT)* display in which the electron beam paints the face of the tube (*screen*) line-by-line, thus creating the image.

**raster graphics** - Computer graphics that will be displayed on a *pixel*-based *raster display device*. Pixel selection may be accomplished in *real-time* by free-hand *input* drawn with a *stylus* or a *mouse*.

**raster scan** - A *video display* technique in which the electron beam scans across the surface of the screen in a regular pattern, illuminating *phosphors* according to the contents of the *frame buffer*.

**raw stock** - Unexposed, unprocessed film stock.

**ray tracing** - A technique to generate an image from a geometric model of an object. For each *pixel* in an image, one or more theoretical rays are cast from the viewer's eyepoint into the model, to determine what part of the model should be displayed at that point in the resulting image. The key feature of *ray tracing* is that the ray through each pixel is allowed to reflect or refract off, or through, any surface encountered to simulate a true optical ray. In general, each ray breaks into two at each surface (the part reflected and the part transmitted), which is why ray tracing computations can grow exponentially. Years of effort have gone into finding efficient (non-exponential) *algorithms* that give the same optical effects as ray tracing (which is really just brute-force optics). Unlike *radiosity*, ray tracing is good for calculating *specular reflection* and refraction.

**read only memory (ROM)** - Non-adjustable *memory* which is usually used to store permanent information that is accessed repeatedly. Usually written when manufactured for use as reference data by a *computer*, in contrast to *memory* which is designed to be constantly changed and updated for transient *programs* and *data*. Most computers have a *ROM* that tells them what to do when the power is first switched on. See also, *CD-ROM*.

**real time** - performance of a computerized operation that gives the impression of instantaneous response, ie: displaying an image or responding to the user's request immediately following its occurrence.

**real time image generation** - Results when the performance of the computations necessary to update the image is completed within the *refresh rate*, so that the sequence appears correct and natural to the viewer, ie: once every 1/30th of a second for video display.

**rear projection** - An image projected onto a screen located between the *projector* and the foreground action, and ultimately the camera. Used for the purpose of combining previously photographed or recorded material with the objects or people in the foreground, between the screen and the camera.

**reconstruction** - The regeneration of information from some abstraction of it. eg: producing an image of a human pelvis from data provided from a *CT* scan. Also, the conversion of a two-dimensional image into a three-dimensional image.

**record** - A group of related fields of information in a *database*, treated as a single unit.

**recursion** - The use of something to define itself, eg: see, *recursion*.

**reduced instruction set computing (RISC)** - A technology for high-performance *processor* design which increases a *CPU's*, or a *computer's* operating speed by running it with a limited (reduced) set of instructions for the performance of the various tasks. Because the instructions imbedded in the circuitry of these streamlined chips are simpler, and relatively few in number, they take less time to execute.

**redundancy** - The use of multiple *devices* to increase reliability. Using *parallel processing* to increase reliability as opposed to increasing speed or throughput can be considered *redundancy*.

**reflection map** - A representation of an environment that is mapped onto an object to simulate reflection. See, *mapping*.

**reflectance model** - Function which describes light on a surface by making assumptions concerning light sources, angles, surface texture, etc. Also called "illumination model".

**refraction map** - A mapping technique which deals with refractions and transparencies. See, *mapping*.

**refractive index** - A measure of the difference between the speed of light in different transparent media. Used in ray tracing to calculate refraction.

**refresh** - Rewriting (scanning) an image onto the *display screen* to *refresh* the *phosphors* so as to maintain a constant image. Typically, the rate at which the image must be generated to avoid *flicker* is 30-60 cycles per second.

**refresh rate** - The number of frames drawn on the screen per second, giving the rate at which the *display* is regenerated.

**refresh vector display** - See, *vector display*.

**register** - A *memory* location which is fast and close to a *processor*, as compared to the main memory *storage*.

**registration** - The alignment of features from two images.

**relational database** - A *database* management system (*DBMS*) that allows *data* to be accessed based on relationships set up among several database files.

**remote sensing** - The capture of information from a distance. eg: the use of satellites to photograph the earth.

**remote terminal** - A *computer terminal* which communicates with a larger *computer*. It may or may not have local processing capability.

**rendering** - The conversion of the geometry, coloring, texturing, lighting etc of a scene, as described by the modeling process, into colored *pixels* for display.

**RenderMan** - An industry *standard* for high-quality, photorealistic three-dimensional scene description and image information transfer. Developed by *Pixar* and gaining widespread acceptance and use.

**repeatability** - The capability of a computerized *motion control* camera system, or a *computer animation* system, to repeat a move with optimum accuracy.

**requestor** - A bounded region on a *screen* used to give information to a *tool*, selected action or *animation* usually in response to a programmed request. eg: a request for a **yes** or **no** answer on whether to overwrite an existing file during a *save* function.

**resolution** - 1> For *raster scan* display systems, the number of *pixels* per line together with the number of scan lines per frame, or the number of pixels per inch or unit of area. A display which can accommodate a larger number of pixels per area therefore is capable of producing an image with more detail, and thus has a higher *resolution*.
2> For images, *resolution* refers to the size of the *pixel array* needed to represent an entire image. This is often much greater than the *screen* resolution.
3> The smallest distance between two elements which can be perceived as distinct by the viewer.
4> The smallest distance between two elements which can be resolved by the photographic emulsion on a film.

**restart capability** - The ability to recover from a failure at that point in the *program* where the *computer* failed, as opposed to having to run the whole program again from the beginning.

**retrace** - Return of the electron beam to the left side or top of the screen after a horizontal or vertical scan.

**reveal** - The transitional effect of revealing more and more of a scene or image with each additional frame. See also, *wipe*.

**reverse display** - A *display screen* that can be instructed to reverse the natural display lighting sequence so as to show either dark characters on a light background, or light characters on a dark background.

**RGB** - Red, Green, Blue. Often used to refer to a type of video color encoding scheme, and the type of color *monitor* that displays it. In *RGB*, a color is defined as percentages of red, green and blue, the additive *primaries*. See also, *CMY*.

**right-reading** - An image is considered *right-reading* when the *type* reads normally from left to right.

**ring structure** - A simple way of linking *processors* together in a circular pattern. Only two connections are required per processor, but it can take a long time to get information to the opposite side of a large *ring*.

**RIO** - Resolution Independent Object-oriented software. The design and layout module of AT&T's SoftVisions graphics software package for *PC* based systems.

**ripple** - An image distorted to give an effect similar to a flag waving in a breeze, or a dream-like effect.

**RISC** - *Reduced Instruction Set Computer*.

**ROM** - *Read Only Memory*.

**rotating in perspective** - The rotation of an image on a selected axis so that its parts maintain *perspective* as they are revealed. As the image is rotated on an axis, information behind the primary image appears smaller, and information before it becomes larger, giving the effect of a natural, three-dimensional object in *screen space*.

**rotation** - The pivoting, or rotation of an image around its central point, or axis.

**rotations** - The pivoting, or rotating of an object around any axes.

**rotoscoping** - Frame-by-frame projection of a live-action scene, or any other previously shot footage, to trace its specific motion. Used to position special effects or graphics into the projected footage, or to create drawn *animation* with a life-like motion.

**rough cut** - An early review version print or recording of a production, done at a stage between the assembly of the various sequences and the finally edited copy of a production. Often assembled without all the various effects in place, or edited to the exact timing.

**routine** - A set of instructions for the *computer* to perform a certain function or task. See also, *subroutine*.

**RS-232** - An *interface* standard for asynchronous data communications between two devices.

**rubber banding** - An *interactive* technique for moving one end of a straight line on a *graphics* or *animation display* while the other remains fixed, or moving a point(s) in the middle of the line while both ends remain fixed.

**rubber stamp** - The ability to duplicate an electronically drawn object on other parts of the *screen*, as many times as desired, through a single, simple command.

**runtime** - The amount of time, in cycles of activity, that it takes for a *computer* to carry out a particular command. Most commonly used to mean "at the time of execution", ie: when the program is run, rather than "at the time of compilation" (compiletime), ie: when the program is formed, or created.

**SAA** - System Application Architecture.

**sample** - A measurement made at a particular instant in space and time, according to a specified procedure.

**sampling rate** - Frequency at which points are recorded, such as in digitizing an image.

**sans serif** - Type forms without *serifs*, the short line or stroke projecting horizontally from the ends of the main stroke of a letter. eg: letters without, or "Sans Serif" compared to letters "With Serifs".

**SAS** - Skeleton Animation System. A *computer animation* system oriented towards human motion, developed by D Zeltzer in 1982, at Ohio State University.

**saturation** - The degree to which a color is undiluted by white light. A color that is 100 percent *saturated* contains no white light.

**save** - To copy something to a file or *disc*.

**scalar machine** - A *computer* which is designed to operate on one instruction at a time. The first commercial computers were *scalar machines*, and this still, by far, the dominant type of computer in use today.

**scalar processing** - Computing with one instruction at a time. Conceptually the simplest way to execute *programs*, it is also the least efficient.

**scale** - In *computer graphics*, the reduction or enlargement of an object.

**scaling** - A function that multiplies the size of an element by a constant value. Enlarging or reducing the number of *pixels* that define an image.

**scan and paint** - A common type of *computer* assisted *animation* in which the outline artwork is created in traditional frame-by-frame style by an artist with pencil and paper. It is then digitized into a computer, filled (painted) digitally, and digitally composited over a digitised, or computer painted, background. As opposed to *computer animation* systems which automatically *interpolate* (*inbetween*) *keyframes* drawn on the computer display.

**scan conversion** - Converting an image into individual scan lines to enable rendering.

**Scanimate** - One of the first *analog computer animation* systems, developed in the early 1970s by Computer Image Corporation. In use by several computer animation production companies until the mid-'80s, *Scanimates* were the first commercially viable computer animation devices. See also, *CAESAR*.

**scanline** - A line composed of individual *pixels* drawn on a *raster*.

**scanline buffer** - See, *frame buffer*.

**scanner** - Equipment for "reading" images and type, differentiating their values, and recording them electronically.

**scanning** - The process of "writing" or "drawing" a *raster* image on a *monitor's screen* by successively addressing points on the display surface.

**scene simulation** - A *computer* generated *background* in which live action characters, or objects, move about realistically through the use of video matting techniques.

**scheduling** - Assigning multiple tasks to available resources. Scheduling problems arise in computing at every level from waiting for the multiplier to finish an operation, to seeing if the whole *computer* is available for the next use.

**scientific computing** - Computing characterized by a requirement for large memory capacity and fast high-*precision, floating-point* operations. It contrasts with Business Computing, which depends more on *I/O* and fixed-decimal-point operations.

**scientific visualization** - Using *computer graphics* and *animation* techniques to give a researcher the ability to see on a *screen* a representation of numerical data generated by a scientific process, possibly using a *supercomputer*.

**scissoring** - The technique of not showing the total frame on the *display screen*, even though the *CRT's* beam continues to, in effect, paint the remainder of the scene off-screen. As opposed to *clipping*. See also, *blanking*.

**SciViz** - Scientific Visualization. Also used, SiViz, SciVi.

**score** - Music written out or printed on *score* paper, the parts for all the different instruments appearing above each other. In film/video use referring to the music track, or theme, or background music for an artistic production.

**screen** - A surface onto which an image is projected by beams of light or electrons, and which is capable of reflecting that image so it can be seen by the human eye. The image can be projected from either the front, or back, of the screen. See also, *front projection, rear projection*.

**screen resident menu** - Function and color controls that appear solely on the *screen*, either the one being used to display the image being created, or on a separate, dedicated, *monochrome* screen. The *menu* appearing on screen space may correspond to a blank space on the *digitizing tablet*, allowing items to be selected with a *stylus*, as well as from the *keyboard*.

**screen size** - The dimensions of the face, or *screen*, of a *cathode ray tube (CRT)*, or other *display device*, as it appears mounted in its housing. Either given as width and height measurements, or as is usually the case for television and video monitors, measured diagonally.

**screen (or image) space** - The two-dimensional coordinate space representing the display surface. Sometimes also used to refer to the three-dimensional space represented by the image, or scene, displayed on a *computer's screen*, as seen from the viewer's eyepoint. See also, *world space*.

**scroll, scrolling** - Movement of an image, or a block of text, across a screen, either up or down, or from side to side. New parts of the image or text are revealed at the opposite edge of the screen from that which the image or text exits.

**SCS** - Shanghai Computer Society.

**SDL** - Screen Descriptive Language.

**SECAM** - Systeme Electronique Couleur Avec Memoire (or Sequential Color with Memory System). A video/television color encoding scheme used in France, the USSR, and other eastern European countries. Characterized by 625 lines per frame at 50Hz.

**section** - A cut-through view, or cross-section, of an object.

**segue** - A visual or audio transition. More than a *dissolve*, it was originally used as a direction in music, meaning to proceed without pause from one theme to another.

**selective object rendering** - To selectively give various rendered surfaces (eg: *bump-mapping, texture-mapping, Gouraud shading*) to different objects in a scene.

**sequencer** - That portion of a *processor* that controls the sequence in which a *program* is executed.

**sequential memory (storage)** - *Data* stored in a linear mode, as in a string of codes on a tape. Often less expensive than *random access* memory, but the time needed to access the material usually takes longer. Also known as serial memory.

**serial interface** - A method of sending printing codes from a *computer* to a *printer* or other *device*, in which one *bit* of information is transferred at a time. This is usually slower than a *parallel interface*.

**serial port** - A communications *device* which can send or receive a stream of information, one *bit* at a time.

**serial processing** - Handling *data* or instructions sequentially.

**serial sectioning** - Creating a three-dimensional screen object in parts, which lets the *computer* program a smooth join.

**serif** - A short light line or stroke projecting horizontally from the ends of the main stroke of a Roman style letter (as opposed to arabic or oriental style characters). Originally, in handwritten letters, a beginning or finishing stroke of the pen. See, *sans serif*.

**service bureau** - A company that processes *computer data* for other organizations on a commercial basis.

**shading** - Techniques used to render an object, based on how light sources are positioned and how they illuminate the object. (See, *flat*, *Gouraud*, *Phong* and *smooth* shading).

**shape** - Refers to two-dimensional entities. See also, *matrix shape*, *object*.

**shared logic system** - A configuration of *word processors* or work stations in which each *terminal* shares a single *CPU*, permitting greater storage capacity and reduced costs. Often the connections are via a *LAN*.

**sharpening filter** - A procedure for sharpening an image which enhances details. The opposite of *diffusion filter*. Also known as a *high-pass filter*.

**shear transformation** - The displacing of part of an object in one direction while another part is displaced in the opposite direction.

**shift register** - *Data* storage which behaves much like a conveyor belt. As data is extracted from one end of a list of numbers (or written into the other end), all the numbers move down one location, allowing the process to be rapidly repeated.

**SIGGRAPH** - Special Interest Group, **Graphics**, of the *Association for Computing Machinery (ACM)*. Convenors of the *SIGGRAPH* conference and exhibition for computer scientists, artists and others interested in computer graphics, held annually in North America. The largest, best known organization and conference for the computer graphics discipline.

**signal processing** - Using a *computer* to clarify or interpret a stream of *data*, such as a sound, or a video, or radio signal.

**silicon** - The basic, most widely used material for the construction of *computer chips* (processing, memory, etc). Used because of its great physical, chemical and electrical stability and non-conductivity.

**SIMD** - *Single Instruction Multiple Data.*

**simultaneous contrast** - Changes in the appearance of a color depending on its background or adjacent colors.

**simultaneous output** - Typing text into a *computer system* and printing it at the same time, without either function affecting the other.

**simulation** - Using a *computer* to imitate some physical process, or natural phenomon, either to substitute for experiment, or to validate a theory of how that process works.

**single frame animation** - Visuals recorded on film or videotape in individual frame increments, or "frame-by-frame".

**single instruction multiple data (SIMD)** - A *parallel processing* scheme, or *computer* architecture that allows multiple data streams to be manipulated based on a single instruction stream. Easier to program than *MIMD*, but limited in complexity of employable *algorithms*.

**Sketchpad** - The first *interactive*, well known, *computer graphics* system, developed by Ivan Sutherland in 1963. The precursor of today's style of geometry-based computer graphics systems.

**skip frame** - The process of speeding-up the action in a sequence by only recording every second, or third *frame*.

**slit scan** - A film technique in which only a portion of an image is photographed at a time, through a moving slit which is scanned across the scene. This effect was one of the first commercially available *computer animation* effects. It was pioneered by John Whitney Sr using an *analog computer system*.

**slope** - The orientation of a *line* on a *plane*.

**Smalltalk** - Legendary research project at Xerox Park, which developed the *WIMP* environment.

**smart terminal** - A terminal with local processing capability. See also, *intelligent terminal, dumb terminal*.

**smooth scroll** - To move a screen image one row or, column, of *pixels* at a time.

**smooth shading** - Techniques that smooth over the facet edges of a *polygon* based *shaded* object, so the resulting surfaces look smooth. See also, *Gouraud* and *Phong* shading.

**SNA** - Systems Network Architecture. *IBM's* communications architecture that defines physical connections, *protocols*, and procedures for all IBM *computers* and *devices*.

**SOFTCEL** - A *computer animation* system that replaces hand drawing and painting onto *cels* by computer operations. Developed by G Stern in 1979, at *NYIT*. See also, *scan and paint*.

**soft copy** - The images generated on the face of a *computer display screen*. Not being "hard", they will disappear when new *data* is presented for display.

**software** - A *program*, or collection of programs, including utility routines and operating systems, which controls the operations of a *computer*.

**Sogitec** - One of the early leaders among European (France) *developmental computer animation* production facilities, it merged with *TDI's* production department in early 1989 to form *Ex Machina*.

**solids modeling** - Creating a three-dimensional representation of an object on a *computer display* screen, using mathematical models that describe objects as occupying a volume. Most representations used in three-dimensional computer graphics are surface models that only describe the surface of the object. eg: B-REP (boundary representation) vs CSG (computational solid geometry).

**solid state** - A broad family of electronic devices made solely of solid materials which control current without the use of moving parts, heated filaments or vacuum gaps.

**solid state disc** - Fast mass *storage device* with no moving parts, providing fast access and near zero latency.

**sound effects** - Noises and sounds for a film other than speech or music.

**source code** - A *program* before it is translated into machine code, or *binary*, eg: a *Fortran* source. These are the source instructions used to write a program, or a specific collection of *software*, which contain the basic set-up instructions for that program's operation. Without knowing the *source code* used to write the program, it is very difficult to copy, modify or add-to that program. See also, *code*.

**source language** - The *language* used by a *programmer* to write a *program*. Note: *code* usually refers to the program itself, *language* refers to the actual language the code is written in.

**SPARC** - Scalable Processor Architecture. Sun Microsystems' version of *RISC*, which is independent of implementation technology. This technology is being licensed to other *chip* makers.

**spatial** - Having the attributes of two- or three-dimensional space.

**spatial data** - Usually refers to distribution of a variable, or the relationship between variables in a geographic region. Topographical data and demographic features are examples of information readily represented *spatially*, ie: on a map.

**spatial frequency** - A mathematical construct roughly corresponding to how often shapes appear, or can appear, in an image. Small shapes have high *spatial frequencies*.

**spatial resolution** - The number of *pixels* used to represent an image from side-to-side and top-to-bottom.

**special effects animation** - Animation of visual effects such as smoke, water, un-natural phenomenon.

**spectral color** - Color of a single wavelength on the visible portion of the electromagnetic spectrum. Refraction of white light yields the spectral hues ranging from violet, with the shortest wavelength, through blue, green, yellow, and orange, ending with red at the longest wavelength. Black, white and colors which are mixtures of wavelengths are not *spectral colors*. Note: video, film and print are incapable of spectral colors, lasers are classified by the spectral color they emit.

**spectral energy distribution** - A diagram showing the component wavelengths of a color, as measured by a *spectrometer*.

**spectrometer** - Device for measuring the wavelengths of a color, giving its *spectral energy distribution*.

**specular reflections** - Reflections that are not uniformly distributed, and which therefore create highlights on an object's surface. See also, *Phong shading*.

**spherical coordinates** - See, *polar coordinates*.

**spline** - A type of mathematical model used to represent curves. *Splines* are usually implemented as *polygons* with a large number of very small sides. The importance of splines is that they give very smooth curves for a very small human input - namely, the sparsely separated knots. See *NURBS*.

**spot size** - the diameter of the spot produced by the beam on the face of a *CRT*.

**spreadsheet** - A *software tool* for financial analysis and the planning and manipulation of financial *data*. *Spreadsheet* is the accounting term for rows and columns of financial data.

**sprite** - A *pixel array* that is smaller than the total area of the picture, and functions as a sub-module. Common in games animation.

**squash** - The foreshortening of an object, or character, in animation to give the illusion that it is decelerating within the scene. See also, *stretch*.

**stair-steps** - See, *aliasing, anti-aliasing*.

**stand alone system** - An integrated unit which includes *input, processing, storage*, and *output*, is not linked to any other equipment, and can perform its functions independently. eg: a graphics workstation with its own *keyboard, digitizing tablet, printer* and *video recorder*, as opposed to a *terminal* online to a *computer*.

**stand-in** - See *bounding box*.

**standards conversion** - The conversion of video/television display signals between the *NTSC, PAL* and/or *SECAM* broadcast standards.

**star field** - The representation of stars in outer space, with the viewer seemingly moving through them. A popular *computer animation* effect.

**status register** - A storage location, usually close to, or a part of, the control *processor*, which holds indicators of the machine state; whether the last operation produced an overflow, whether the memory location just read contained a one-*bit* error, etc.

**stencil** - A *paint system* function that serves as either a positive, or negative, mask to protect a certain part of a screen image when the rest of the image is being further manipulated.

**STEP** - Standard for the Exchange of Product Model Data. An international standard being developed for the exchange of computer image data.

**step-frame** - Using a computerized video editor to delete certain frames in a recorded video sequence, causing kinetic, strobe-like movement.

**stereo imagery** - True three-dimensional imagery, which is generated in pairs. To see the *stereo* effect requires special projection and viewing equipment.

**stereopsis** - The dimensional perception resulting from two different views of the same image.

**stet** - Proofreader's term to ignore indicated corrections, ie: "leave as is".

**still store** - A *memory* device that can file, in digital form, a large number of single *frames* of video, which may then be recalled sequentially or randomly as needed.

**stop frame** - The process of recording single *frames*, one at a time, as they are computed. As it generally takes a period of time to compute each frame, this is usually not a *real time* process, as it is with live-action recording (or filming).

**storage tube** - *A cathode ray tube (CRT)* whose screen surface will retain an image for a long period of time.

**storyboard** - A form of shooting script consisting of a series of sketches of various key scenes/frames, in sequence, with appropriate dialogue and sound effects written below them. A method of scripting an animation production and showing how a it will look before production starts.

**stretch** - The elongation of an object, or character, in animation, to give the illusion that it is accelerating within the scene. See also, *squash*.

**strobing** - A peculiar jitter effect that results in *computer animation* when an object is moved too fast, and leaves a representative trail behind it. Often done intentionally for the visual effect. It is *temporal aliasing* (*aliasing* in time), the equivalent to *jaggies*, which are aliasing in space.

**stylus** - The inkless, electronic pen used with a *digitizing tablet*, or *touchscreen menu*, to draw free-hand artwork or initiate computer system commands from the menu.

**subroutine** - Specialized function that can be used with, and called-up by, an existing high-level *language*. Also known as procedure or function in some languages.

**subroutine library** - A collection of *subroutines*.

**subscript** - A small symbol, numeral or type that prints below and to the side of another character, as in scientific notations.

**subtitle** - A title, text or message superimposed on a *frame*, or several frames, of a film or video. Usually at the bottom of the frame, but this position is not mandatory.

**super** - Television industry slang for *superimpose*. Usually used in reference to *supering* text, product information, pricing or a *logo* over the action in the frame(s).

**super black** - *Luminance* level below normal video black, used to set-up *keying*.

**supercomputer** - A very fast, high capacity *mainframe computer* which has significantly higher performance that the other computers of its generation. The world's fastest computers.

**superimpose** - To lay one image, or portion of an image, over another. The "top" image can be either opaque or have various degrees of transparency. In television/video parlance, to *super* refers to the keying of text or title over the screen image. A *super* is also the name given to the title or image being *superimposed* over the scene or frame.

**Superpaint** - The first true *digital paint system*, developed by Richard Shoup in 1973, which was used, in 1976, to produce the first computer animation images ever used as part of a national (USA) television broadcast, and for which Shoup and Superpaint won an Emmy.

**superscript** - A small symbol, numeral or type that prints above, and to the side of another character.

**surface mount technology** - A manufacturing method which allows more *chips* to occupy a given area of a *circuit board*.

**surface model** - A way to design three-dimensional objects by manipulating a curved grid, or group, of *polygons*. Also known as Boundary Representation, or B-REP.

**surface normal** - See, *normal*.

**surface patch modeling** - An alternative modeling process to *polygonal*, in which even a sphere is composed of numerous small flat surfaces. In *surface patch modeling* the surface is defined in the *computer* as a series of control points, which act like tensioning points on a rubber band. Very adept at creating convex or concave surfaces.

**surface rendering** - The process of generating images of three-dimensional objects from a set of mathematically defined surfaces. A technique used by traditional *computer graphics* systems for representing objects, it shows only surface features and is incapable of representing internal contents of the model.

**sustained MFLOPS** - Also called "Application *MFLOPS*" or "Job MFLOPS". The speed which a *computer* achieves in actual use, as contrasted with *peak MFLOPS*.

**symbolic processing** - The use of tools and techniques developed in the field of *AI* to represent large bodies of knowledge. *Symbolic processing* uses *data* structures appropriate to a specific problem rather than representing data numerically. It is used for a broad range of applications such as *expert systems* and *rapid prototyping*, as well as applications found in conventional computing, such as numerical computation and graphics.

**sync** - Refers to synchronous, *synchronization* or synchronizing.

**sync generator** - A device that generates the horizontal and vertical *sync* signals in video.

**synchronization** - The process of maintaining two or more scanning processes in phase. In filmmaking, a timing reference to which the initiation of an activity is linked, eg: the combining of speech, effects and music tracks with the video or filmed activity so they are in synchronization with the action.

**synchronous communications** - When an entire block of *data*, such as a full screen, is transmitted at one time. The data is usually preceded by several synchronisation *bytes* that synchronize the transmitter and receiver, and a special "start-of-text" (STX) byte, and it is usually followed by a special "end-of-text" (ETX) byte. Fewer overhead, or non-data bits are transmitted with *synchronous* than with *asynchronous communication*, so the communications line is used much more efficiently.

**Synthavision** - A *computer animation* system based on the manipulation of solid shapes and *ray-casting*, developed and used by *MAGI*.

**system** - An integrated assembly of *hardware* and *software* designed to implement a given application or set of applications.

**Tagged Image File Format (TIFF)** - A widely supported format for *scanned images*.

**tank shot** - A shot or sequence photographed in a tank of water, usually with miniatures, but with live actors also, or for other special effects.

**technical director** -The person in a *computer animation* production who is in charge of making sure the *hardware*, and particularly the *software*, can perform the tasks demanded by the *animator*. Often the *technical director* does the required special programming or modifications.

**telecommunications** - Generally used in reference to communications from one *computer terminal* to another via regular voice, or dedicated *data*, telephone lines (although it does refer to all telephone communications).

**teleconferencing** - A general term for conferencing that involves communications links. Based on one-way, two-way or multiple interactive voice transmission of live signals between two or more points. A method of "having a meeting" among people from several locations without them having to physically come together in the same location.

**temporal aliasing** - *Aliasing* in time. See, *strobing*.

**terminal** - A point in a *system,* or in a communications network, at which *data* can be entered, transferred or displayed. See, *dumb terminal*.

**terrain modeling** - A *computer program* to generate realistic-looking natural surfaces, most often through the use of *fractals*.

**terrain rendering** - One of the applications of surface rendering in which enhanced images are used to reconstruct physical terrain from *digital* terrain elevation *data* and image data.

**tessellation** - The division of smooth surfaces into *polygons* that fit together like a mosaic.

**tesseract** - The four-dimensional analog of a cube.

**text mode** - The manner in which text is displayed, ie: normal, italics, bold, subscript etc. In a graphics terminal, either *text mode* or graphics mode must be set-up by the host before corresponding instructions are sent.

**text string** - A limited set of consecutive characters.

**texture mapping** - The utilization of two-dimensional images of surfaces and their textures (eg: wood grain, marble) to give a three-dimensional object a specified "look" or appearance. The two-dimensional texture image is *mapped* onto a three-dimensional object's surface when it is *rendered* by the *computer*. See, *mapping*.

**thermal printing** - A method of printing that uses chemically treated heat-sensitive paper that darkens when a hot *printhead* "burns in" the dot matrix for the type. Although not considered a high-quality method of printing, it is quieter than other forms of printing and lends itself to printing from a continuous roll of paper. Used extensively in *fax* machines.

**thermographic printers** - Printers, particularly color printers, that use heat contact to transfer color pigment from various, or multi-colored ribbons onto the paper. *Thermographic printers* can print fully colored images onto paper just as they appear on a color monitor.

**Thomson Digital Image (TDI)** - Manufacturers of the EXPLORE computer animation software for both *workstations* and *PC* (286/386) based systems. TDI's production department merged, in early 1989, with *Sogitec* to form *Ex Machina*.

**three-axis rotation** - A method of allowing an image to pivot anywhere in space.

**three-dimensional rendering** - The ability to take a *computer*-generated graphic model and assign it properties (ie: colors, textures), describe the location of light sources, and produce a two-dimensional perspective image as seen from a defined point of view.

**thresholding** - A technique used to classify materials within an image. In *thresholding*, ranges of *pixel* intensities, representing the various types of materials, would be selected, and all pixels having values within those ranges would be considered to be the appropriate materials. These ranges, of necessity, are sometimes quite broad, and as a result, thresholding can on occasion result in incorrect classification. It also, typically, causes *aliasing*.

**throughput** - The total amount of useful work performed by a *data processing system* during a given period of time.

**TIFF** - *Tagged Image File Format*.

**time** - The fourth-dimension in *computer animation*. It permits different spatial relationships to be expressed and related, such as in moving images for film/video and animation.

**time-lapse photography** - The technique of single *frame* recording used to visually speed-up extremely slow action. Single frames are recorded at regular, but long-spaced intervals, so that when they are replayed at regular speed, the action, which could have takes several hours, or days, to record, happens in a short enough span for a viewer to readily see what is happening. eg: a flower blooming.

**timesharing** - The sharing of a main *computer* facility by many users, each of whom has a remote terminal. Processing time is "shared" so that users are unaware of each other.

**title** - A series of *frames* in a film or video production consisting of written words giving the name of the production, who produced it, and the principal actors. *Titles* are often shown *superimposed* over live action scenes or other images.

**titler** - Another term for *character generator*.

**Token Ring** - *IBM's* widely used *LAN* technology for *microcomputers*.

**tools-tool kit** - "Ready made" *software* sets which a programmer can use to develop *programs* without having to develop them from scratch, eg: *menus*, forms, *windows*, etc.

**toon** - Character in a **cartoon** *animation*.

**Topas** - Three Dimensional Object Processing and Animation Software. The 3-D *modeling* and *animation software* package for *PC* based systems from AT&T's Graphics Software Labs.

**top-down design** - A methodology for *program* development which prescribes that one deals with general principles first and details last. Although this appears to be a statement of common sense, *programmers* are notorious for avoiding the principle.

**topology** - In general terms, the way things are connected together. eg: the *topology* of a large corporation's organization chart resembles that of the branches of a tree. Also, the name for a brand of analytical geometry.

**touchscreen** - A touch-sensitive terminal *screen* that allows the user to exercise function controls by actually touching the screen, or designated portions of it, either by hand, or with a *stylus*.

**trace** - Scanning path of the beam of a *CRT*.

**track ball** - A ball, recessed into a surface of a *device* provided with sensors such that when it is rotated, the ball provides x and y coordinate information to the *computer*. Similar in operation to a *mouse*, except that the *device* holding the *trackball* remains stationary, ie: a mouse turned upside down.

**tractor drive** - A method of paper transport in which attached continuous sheets of paper, supplied with a series of punched holes down each side, are pulled through the *printer* by sprockets with matching pins, which are usually mounted on a separate "*tractor*" unit attached above the *platen*. If the sprockets are attached to the platen, it is referred to as a *pin feed* (or pin drive) printer. A method of precise, continuous paper transport suitable for high speed printing or long unattended printer runs.

**transaction processing** - The running of a sequence of *database* operations as a single unit of work.

**transfer** - The exchange of material, or *data*, from one medium to another, eg: from film to videotape.

**transformations** - Operations applied to an image *data* base to perform *translation* of axis, *scaling*, *rotation* and *perspective*, accomplished by either *software* or *hardware*. See also, *matrix*.

**translation** - Movement relative to the origin of a coordinate system, or movement of the origin of the coordinate system. To move an object without rotation, usually in a straight line, either left or right, up or down, or in or out, of three-dimensional space.

**transparency** - The degree to which an object transmits light. The opposite of *opacity*. See also, *mapping*.

**transparent** - In programming, *computer* operations of which the user is unaware. The more transparent the program, the easier it is for people who are non-computer literate to use.

**transparent computer animation** - The use of *computer animation* and graphics imaging techniques in creating a scene or an image in film/video production, which is not readily apparent to the viewer as a computer modeled object or computer generated effect, but which enhance the overall visual image, or add to the values of the production.

**transparent data sharing/access** - A characteristic of advanced workgroup computing technology in which a user can retrieve and view *data* regardless of where it is stored within the computing environment.

**transparent overlay** - An overlay plane, which may display menus, etc, through which some of the main frame buffer image can be seen.

**transputer** - A single *chip* which contains a *computer*, *memory*, and communications links, created specially for *parallel processing*. The term was coined by Inmos, the first company to create such a chip.

**travelling matte** - A *matte* that moves with an image, and changes shapes as it does.

**treatment** - An initial description of a film or video production in narrative form, written before the script is prepared.

**tree** - A *data* structure which allows *records*, matrices, single words, or any items of data, to be hierarchically structured.

**triangulate** - To divide *polygons*, or a set of points, into a network of triangles, rather than superimposing a grid structure, ie: to avoid non-planar surfaces, or to break-down complex or concave polygons.

**trichromatic** - Three-colored. In *computer graphics*, *trichromatic* generally refers to the three primary colors, *RGB*.

**Triple I** - A name used to refer to *Information International Inc.*

**tristimulus representation** - A three-variable color description model in which color is described by three separate information channels. The method usually used in implementing color on a *computer*.

**TS** - *Tuple space.*

**tuple** - A sequence of typed fields, used in *tuple space (TS)*.

**tuple space (TS)** - A model for parallel programming. A base *programming language* with the addition of *TS* operations equals a *parallel* programming dialect.

**Turing** - A general purpose *programming language* designed as an alternative for a wide range of languages, from *BASIC* and *Logo* to *Pascal*. Developed at the University of Toronto in 1983, it is named after Alan Turing.

**turn-key system** - A complete *computer system* containing all *hardware* and *software* needed to produce *computer animation*, so all the user needs to do is "turn the key" and it is ready to operate. Also now generally included in the term are complete software packages that can run on a variety of readily available *personal computers* or *workstations*.

**TWEEN** - A *computer animation* system developed by Ed Catmull in 1979, at *NYIT*, which is based on the production and modification of in-betweens. It has since been developed further and is still in use as part of the NYIT software package.

**type** - Generally used to refer to a single, or a group of characters (letters, numerals, symbols) used for mechanically or electronically printing or displaying written material. Also, referring to the written portion of an assembled image. Originally, the actual piece of wood or metal with a letter or numeral carved on one side, which was assembled with other pieces of *type* to form words and lines of type, which were then printed onto paper by the printing press. See also, *typeface*.

**typeface** - The design of a particular set of letters, numerals, symbols and punctuation marks, such as Helvetica or Times Roman.

**typeface family** - A family of alphabets based on a common design theme. Helvetica is the family name, Helvetica Condensed is the name of one style in the Helvetica family.

**ULSI** - Ultra large scale integration *chip*.

**undercrank** - A film technique for speeding up the action of a scene by filming it at a speed slower than the standard 24 frames per second.

**uninterruptable power supply (UPS)** - Battery back-up devices that are located between a *computer, device,* or other piece of equipment, and the main electrical power supply. Should the main power fail, they instantly begin to supply power from their batteries to prevent unintentional equipment shut down, which in computers can mean the loss of work-in-progress and *memory.* Most *UPS* are designed for limited back-up use, their main function being to give the user time to correctly *save* work and shut down the equipment in an orderly, prescribed fashion. They also are designed to act as *line filters*, filtering the main power on a continuing basis.

**Unix** - An operating system created by AT&T's Bell Labs in 1969, long popular in university, and scientific environments, now gaining rapid acceptance in the business community. *Unix* offers true multitasking, fast graphics and sophisticated networking, making it particularly well suited to the needs of *computer graphics* and *animation.*

**upper case** - Capital letters.

**UPS** - *Uninterruptable power supply.*

**user friendly** - *Programs* in which the user is provided instructions or prompting for performing most operations. Also, refers to the application of human factors knowledge to the design of equipment to make it easier to use, a branch of *AI.*

**user interface** - The means by which a *computer* and a user communicate. It is the collection of everything the user sees, hears and does while activating the computer to perform some task. Also known as Computer Human Interface (CHI). See also, *GUI.*

**utility programs** - Support *programs* used to help operate a *computer* by performing a restricted set of operations, such as assemblers, editors, file conversion programs and debuggers.

**value** - Comparison of a chromatic color to an achromatic color along the grey scale from white to black. Other words used almost synonymously are *brightness, luminosity,* and *luminance.*

**vaporware** - A derogatory term for a product, usually *software,* that is announced before it is ready for sale, or in some cases, even before it exists.

**VAR** - Value added reseller, or re-marketer. Usually a company that writes or modifies *software,* or both, and sells it in combination with *hardware* as a single package. A *VAR* can be any company that adds value to a product in preparing it for resale.

**variable name** - The English language *mnemonic* that is usually used by a *computer* to reference anything in *storage.* Words referenced by names are called "*variables*". A variable is also a name that is used symbolically in place of the specific *address* of an item of *data.*

**VAX/VMS** - An operating system from Digital Equipment Corporation (DEC). VAX is a family of superminicomputers. VMS means virtual memory system.

**vector** - An entity that possesses the attributes of magnitude and direction, a line. On a *plane,* a straight line (*vector*) is defined by two *points,* or a point, a direction and a magnitude, ie: the normal form of line equation.

**vector display** - *Storage tube* in which the electron beam writes lines on the surface of the *cathode ray tube (CRT)* from one defined point to another. The beam can be repositioned while it is turned off, or it can draw a line when it is moved to another position while turned on.

**vector generator** - A function generator which in hardware takes vector definition data, typically x and y beam displacements, or end point coordinates, and draws a line directly on the screen. See *Digital Differential Analyser.*

**vector graphics** - The branch of *computer graphics* that deals with line drawings. Images are represented as line segments (vectors) rather than as shaded images. It pre-dates the widespread availability of *raster* graphics *display* technology.

**vector machine** - A *computer* which is designed to rely heavily on *vector processing* methods to achieve high performance. *Vector machines* are more economical to build than *scalar machines* of the same performance, but impose constraints on the *programmer* wishing to make good use of the hardware.

**vector processing** - Using the same operation for a list of numbers. Both *parallel* and pipeline techniques are effective for *vector processing.*

**vector registers** - Special *storage* locations close to a *computer's* processing unit (*CPU*), which permit entire lists of numbers to be used in the computer's "scratchpad" calculations, as if they were single entities.

**vectorize** - To reorganize a program so as to reveal repetitious operations.

**vertex/vertices** - A point in space defined by its x, y, and z coordinates. Also, the corner points of a *polygon* are called *vertices*.

**Vertigo V2000** - A *workstation*-based computer animation system utilizing proprietary processing boards, now manufactured by Cubicomp.

**very-large-size integration (VLSI)** - The technology of building several hundred thousand *devices* onto a single *chip*. High density *memories* and fast *microprocessors* are among the best known achievements of *VLSI* technology.

**VGA** - Video graphics array. A graphics display standard used with *personal computers*, which is replacing *EGA*.

**VideoCel** - A three-dimensional *computer animation* program, developed by Thomas Klimek in 1976, and used during its operation by Computer Creations Inc.

**videodisc** - A large capacity image storage medium that uses a *laser* to read *digital* or *analog data* that is encoded on its surface. See *CD-ROM*.

**video display** - Television type *display* (ie: raster format), which uses an analog signal. A *digital-to-analog (DAC)* converter transforms the digital information from a *computer,* to a video signal that is used in the display.

**video merge** - Using the *alpha channel* to determine the mix of video signals from two independent *frame store* processors.

**video synthesizer** - A device for modifying video images in *real time*. See *Scanimate*.

**videotext** - Television transmission of printed text and graphics information, usually used in consumer-based interactive television transmission, such as general data/information systems. A branch of *electronic publishing*.

**viewpoint** - The position of the viewer's eye relative to a model or scene. See also, *point-of-view*.

**virtual device interface** - A *software program* that allows different models of graphics *computers* to talk to each other.

**virtual memory** - A technique for extending a *computer's* internal random access memory by exchanging portions of its *RAM* with a *disc* storage unit, trading it back and forth so fast that the machine apparently, or virtually, has much more main memory. *Virtual memory* permits the use of programs that are larger than the computer's internal memory. Originally used in *mainframes* and minicomputers, its use is spreading to smaller computers.

**ViSC** - Visualization in Scientific Computing.

**VISIONS** - A three-dimensional *computer animation* system developed by Judson Rosebush, and others, in 1975. Used originally by Digital Effects, it is now being further developed and used by Rosebush Visions.

**Vista Vision** - A motion picture format similar to standard 35mm still photography format, in which the frames are positioned horizontally along the length of the film. Each frame covers the area of two standard Academy frames, producing twice the image resolution of standard movie film.

**visual display terminal (VDT)** - A *device* which usually includes a *keyboard*, *cathode ray tube (CRT)* for displaying text, and a *memory*, or storage area. *VDTs* can be stand-alone units accepting various kinds of *input*, or can operate *on-line* to a host computer. They are used for a number of purposes, such as *word processing* and file management.

**VLSI** - *Very-large-scale integration chip.*

**VM/CMS** - Virtual machine/conversational monitor system. A widely used *IBM operating system, especially in timesharing applications.*

**VME bus** - A *data* communication system used within some *computers*.

**volume** - An object that fills a three-dimensional space. A solid ball is a *volume*, since it fills space. This is distinct from its surface, which is infinitely thin and thus does not fill space, even though it exists in three dimensions.

**volume element (Voxel)** - The smallest three-dimensional area of volume which has meaningful information associated with it, in effect, a three-dimensional *pixel*. In practical application, *voxels* are evenly spaced in a three-dimensional *array*.

**volume rendering** - As opposed to *surface rendering*, a set of procedures to generate images of *data* that is volumetric in nature. A technique developed by *Pixar* for the creation of an image which shows not just the surfaces of a three-dimensional object, but the contents of the object as well. The interior details being visualized may be physical, such as bone and muscle in a human body, or the structure of a machine part, or they may be other characteristics such as fluid flow, heat or stress.

**volume visualization** - The creation of a three-dimensional visualization of *data*, including both the surface and interior elements of an object.

**Voxel** - *Volume element.*

**Warnock's algorithm** - The area-subdivision algorithm for polygon rendering developed by John Warnock at the University of Utah in 1969, noted for its relative computational simplicity.

**warping** - The transformation of an image in a complex manner that may result in the image being twisted and enlarged in some areas and reduced in others.

**Watkins' algorithm** - An algorithm for removing hidden surfaces, developed by GS Watkins in 1971.

**wave equation** - An important equation in mathematical physics that describes the way disturbances propagate through a medium. *Computer simulations* of the *wave equation* are useful in modeling such things as seismic exploration *data* and supersonic airfoils.

**Wavefront** - A widely used, workstation based, three-dimensional *computer animation* system produced by Wavefront Technologies, USA.

**weather system** - A *computer animation* and *screen* display system linked to a radar, satellite, or weather-data service, usually used for broadcast television weather reports.

**wedge** - A testing procedure which is a critical step in Special Effects and *computer animation* work. The images, or sample *frames*, are recorded at various exposure levels and through various filters to determine the proper "look". Unlike *live action* sequences where a light meter can be used to determine lighting and exposure levels, special effects and computer animation often must be finalized while still "in production" in the computer.

**weight** - In reference to *type*, the relationship between a letter's own solid strokes and its open spaces. A letter is said to be "light" if the strokes are thin, "heavy" if the strokes are thick.

**white space** - That part of printed matter which is not covered by *type* and illustrations. An element of graphic design.

**widow** - A single word, or part of a word, in a line by itself at the end of a paragraph. Also; a word, or part of a word, standing alone in one line of heading, an extremely short last line in a caption.

**width value table** - The list of widths assigned to all characters in a given font.

**WIMP** - Window Manager, Icons, Mice and Pop-up Menus. The now standard *user interface* design developed at Xerox Park, and popularized by Apple Computer's Lisa and Macintosh systems. See also, *Smalltalk*.

**Winchester disc** - A very common type of *hard disc* storage device suitable for use with *minicomputers*, *personal computers* and *workstations*. It has set the pattern for the many hard disc devices now available. The term *"Winchester disc"* is often used to refer to hard discs in general.

**window(s)** - *Software* generated space(s) (or *window*) on a *computer display* screen, usually of variable size, that allows the user to see several functions at once on a single screen. These function *windows* can be related to the same *program*, or they can be used to facilitate the running of two or more programs at the same time.

**wipe** - Identical to a *reveal*, however a *wipe* is generally used at the transition between scenes, rather than the transition between images and elements.

**wireframe** - Representation of an object as a see-through, three-dimensional framework consisting only of straight line segments. The name reflects the fact that when these representations are displayed, they appear to be made-up of interconnected wires.

**wireframe object** - An image generated by displaying only the edges of all *polygons*.

**word** - One storage location in *memory* or on a *peripheral device*. Usually 8, 12 (not now common), 16, 32, 64, or 128 (in some *mainframes*) *bits* make up a *word*.

**word addressing** - A method of addressing a *computer memory* which reads or writes an entire *word* of *data* all at once, usually made up of 32 or 64 *bits*. *Word addressing* is appropriate for applications where most of the data items of interest take many bits to represent, such as 15-digit numbers. See also, *precision*.

**word processor/processing** - Referring to the use of a *computer*, special *software*, and a *printer* for the writing, processing and manipulation of text matter. Using a *word processing* system, text can be written, stored, re-written, copied, duplicated, portions of it moved within the overall text, exported, spell-checked, formatted and output via a printer in various type forms.

**workgroup** - Best described as a corporate department or division in which *computer* users, usually through the use of a *LAN*, require *data* access and sharing capabilities to carry out their "groups" objectives.

**WORM** - *Write once, read many*.

**workstation** - A full-featured, high performance configuration of *computer* equipment designed to be used by one person at a time, usually in the form of a desk-top or desk-side unit. A *workstation* may be a *terminal* attached to a larger computer, it may be *networked* with other workstations, or it may be a "stand-alone" unit with local processing capability. A workstation generally consists of *input devices (keyboard, mouse, digitizer)*, a *display*, *memory* and *output* devices, such as a *printer, plotter*, or a *video recorder*.

**world space** - The three-dimensional coordinate space where objects interact to make scenes. This is converted by a *perspective transformation* into a two-dimensional space. See also, *image space*.

**write, write to** - The action of recording *data* into a *computer*, or onto a storage *device*.

**write once, read many (WORM)** - Recording *devices* that cannot be erased and re-recorded. A *WORM* can be *written to* once, but the information it contains can be read many times. It usually has a very high capacity for storing information, such as a *CD-ROM* device.

**WYSIWYG** - What you see is what you get. What is shown on a graphic *computer's display* is (usually) what will be printed, plotted or recorded.

**x height** - The height of a lower case letter, exclusive of *ascenders* or *descenders*, such as the letter "x".

**x axis** - The horizontal axis in graphic description.

**Xerography** - The copying of documents onto plain paper using an electrostatic process (ie: Xerox photocopier).

**x, y axes** - The two-dimensional parameters of *image space*.

**x, y, z axes** - The three-dimensional parameters of *world space*. Taken together, they describe the position and/or form of an object in three-dimensional $(x, y, z)$ graphics. Defining points are described according to their position on these axes, and objects can rotate around these axes.

**X.25** - The international standard for packet switched *data* networks.

**X.400** - The international standard for interconnecting *electronic mail* systems.

**y axis** - The vertical axis in graphic description.

**YMCK** - Yellow, Magenta, Cyan and black (written K for "key" separator). A system of colors used for graphic printing. See also, *RGB*.

**z axis** - The depth axis in graphic description.

**z-buffer** - A buffer of *zels* that hold the z-depth of a corresponding *pixel* in a *frame buffer*. Used for *hidden surface removal*. The more *bits*, the greater the precision.

**zel** - Similar to *pixels* as being discrete representations, but instead they represent depth at each point in the image rather than *luminance*.

**ZGRASS** - A high-level *computer animation* system developed by Tom DeFanti in 1983, designed to run on low-cost micro-computer systems, specifically the Datamax UV-1.

**zoom** - Apparent movement of an object closer to, or away from, the viewer.

**zoom axis** - The axis of movement perpendicular to the picture plane.

**zoom lens** - A lens whose focal length can be changed over a wide range.